Ruth
A Study of Life, Loss, and Love

TABLE OF CONTENTS

ABOUT THE AUTHORS

Dr. Jackie Roese grew up in a pagan family in upstate New York. Shortly after coming to Christ, she and her husband Steve moved to Texas to attend Dallas Theological Seminary. Seminary was Jackie's first exposure to Christians, the Bible and the South! After several years of learning, she was brought under the mentorship Dr. Sue Edwards where she was taught to write Bible study materials and teach the Scriptures.

Over the past eight years, she has served as the Teaching Pastor to Women at Irving Bible Church in Irving, Texas. She has taught the Scriptures and trained other women to do the same. In addition, she has envisioned, written and overseen the development of a decade of Bible study materials.

In 2010, Jackie graduated with her Doctorate in Preaching from Gordon Conwell Seminary. It is her desire that women know Jesus through his Word and, in doing so, become more whole as a result. She has a passion to give laywomen the opportunity to develop their teaching skills. From that desiring Jackie felt called to birth The Marcella Project; to transform women to be critical spiritual thinkers and effective teachers of God's Word. Through this ministry women will be challenged to become critical spiritual thinkers about issues pertenent to women, such as body image, sexuality, roles of men and women and more. Along with teaching, writing and training, Jackie also speaks around the U.S. at conferences and retreats.

Jackie resides in Coppell, Texas with her husband, Steve and their three children: Hunter, Hampton and Madison.

ACKNOWLEDGEMENTS

Special thanks to the WE staff at IBC: Julie Pierce, Jodie Niznik, and Nila Odom, for their insight, encouragement, expertise, and support. Cara Martens provided guidance in creative elements. Brianna Barrier Engeler contributed her expertise in theological, content, and copyediting. Kristy Alpert contributed her editing know-how. Lindsey Sobolik was instrumental in design and production. God's best work is done in teams, and this study guide is the result of a collaborative effort. We are grateful for each of you.

WHAT IS THE MARCELLA PROJECT?

The Marcella Project exists to transform women into critical spiritual thinkers & excellent teachers of God's Word. Our Vision is to create a relevant, valued, empowered & enlightened spiritual community of women. We are committed to: Teaching God's Word, Creating a community of believers who think critically about theology, practice and women's spirituality, Preparing women to effectively teach God's Word, Promote women to think critically of theology and practice, Prepare women to teach confidently, and to Proclaim God's Word with relevancy

WHO IS MARCELLA?

Marcella was a woman born 325 AD into a wealthy family in Rome. She became a widow seven months after her marriage. Breaking with convention, she never remarried despite several wealthy suitors' proposals. Her faith drove her to long for simplicity, perhaps even an ascetic lifestyle, yet she chose to honor her mother by living with her in her mansion until she died. She brought many young women into their home to be mentored in the Word and she lived a life of service to the poor.

When St. Jerome, who translated the Scriptures into the Latin Vulgate, came to settle in Rome. Marcella quickly approached him to allow her to become his apprentice. He resisted; she persisted. Jerome finally gave in and Marcella became one of his most capable students and a close confidante. Marcella was known to challenge Jerome's theology more than once. It is said he changed his writings on the words 'amen' and 'alleluia' due to Marcella's theological challenges. When Jerome traveled, he would tell those needing instruction in the Word of God to seek out Marcella.

After her mother's death, Marcella moved out of the mansion and gave her wealth away to those in need. When the barbarians invaded Rome, they captured Marcella and beat her in hopes of getting her to give them her money. They didn't believe her when she explained she had none. After long beatings and no success, they released her. Shortly after, she died as a result of those beatings.

Marcella epitomizes what it means to not succumb to the world's ideal of "what it meant to be a woman," but instead chased after Jesus, letting his love define who she would be. She let nothing get in her way of her pursuit to know God through the Word and to live like Jesus by caring for the poor. Her story challenges us to be "Marcella's" in our world, pursuing Jesus at all costs, even if it means defying our world's ideal of womanhood by allowing our love for Jesus to define who we will be and how we will live.

THE ART OF *RUTH: A STUDY OF LIFE, LOSS, AND LOVE*

Ruth is one of my favorite books of the Bible. Ever since I was a little girl I enjoyed hearing this romantic tale of Ruth finding a wonderful, rich, chivalrous man, falling madly in love, and living happily–ever–after. I even dreamed of a Boaz of my own who would one day sweep me off my feet.

However, a few years ago when Irving Bible Church taught a sermon series on the book of Ruth, I grew to realize that this story is not quite the Cinderella tale I had originally thought. It's a real account about great loss, heartache, hard decisions, and a profound kind of love. Even as I've walked through this book with the authors of this study I've been struck by the immense amount of pain and struggle this story contains. It's a story with loss and brokenness that is all too real for some. Yet God's presence is so rich in the account of Ruth, displaying his faithfulness, goodness, sovereignty, and deep, loyal love.

For the artwork, I chose to illustrate Ruth's themes of heartache and hope by juxtaposing images of death and life with cracked desert ground and fresh daisies. Even in the midst of life's hard and dry times, God can allow love, beauty, and faith to grow. The image is clearly meant to communicate the theme of this study: "Life is hard and God is good." Which, I now believe, is better news to hear than a fairytale any day. This study was a true delight and privilege to design.

—Lindsey Sobolik
Art Director

WHY *RUTH: A STUDY OF LIFE, LOSS, AND LOVE?*

The past several years have been filled with crisis after crisis. From my parents' divorce to sending our teenager away to military school, from my husband's brain tumor to my dad's mental illness . . . the loss of our family business . . . my two best friends leaving our church . . . my chronic back pain . . . and oh yes, the fact that my dog sheds constantly. My world is upside-down, backwards, and sideways. Have you ever been there?

Sometimes in our lives, rounds of difficulties come our way. They hit like a boxer's left hook, making our legs weak and eyes blurred. This is the world we live in — a place where there is beauty, majesty, love, color, pain, and loss. So how do we navigate those times when pain becomes so loud we can't hear anything else?

The book of Ruth provides a window into the lives of two women who are dealing with some really, really hard things. But in the midst of their struggles, God is there; he's got them in his hands. It may be hard to see, but he's in process of caring for their needs and providing a hope and a future. Ruth teaches us the old, but very true axiom that "life is hard, but God is good." I suspect some of us are at a place in our life where that's exactly what we need now: a deep breath and a little hope. *Ruth: A Study of Life, Loss, and Love* is for you. Come join us.

—Jackie Roese
The Marcella Project

HOW TO USE THIS STUDY GUIDE

Women today need Bible study to stay focused and Christ-centered in our busy world.

The questions in this guide will allow you to go as deeply into the material as you like. You may want to finish all of the questions first and then go back to study further as time permits.

Please note that this study of Ruth is expository, meaning that each chapter is covered in depth and in order. However, due to time constraints, some sections have been slightly shortened and a few have been omitted. We would like to encourage you to go back and study through those sections on your own.

Take time to savor the questions, and don't rush through the application. The key to successful Bible study is consistency. Consider spacing your study throughout the week so that you can take time to ponder and meditate on what the Holy Spirit is teaching you.

If you would like to dig more deeply into the lesson and related Scriptures, become familiar with a basic set of Bible study tools. Check out the list of suggested resources in the back of the study for some ideas. Outside resources like a Bible atlas, Bible dictionary, concordance, or commentary will shed new light on the passages you read and study.

Investigate the history, culture, and geography of the time period. Look up parallel passages for additional insight. Don't be afraid to grapple with complex theological issues and differing views. Carefully observe language and punctuation by using an interlinear or comparative Greek-English Bible. Challenge yourself to get the most out of each question. If you have difficulty with a specific question or want more input, feel free to discuss it with your group leader or others in your group.

Come with an anticipation to learn from others and a desire to share yourself and your journey. Give it your best. You will receive the greatest reward of all . . . a deeper relationship with the Creator of the universe and with your sisters in Christ.

GUIDELINES FOR GROUP DISCUSSION

1. To get the most out of the group study sessions, please come prepared and on time. You will offer more, and you won't miss anything. Bring your favorite Bible study tools, like your laptop, a concordance, a Bible dictionary, and more in order to assist in discussion.

2. Respect the value of other women's answers. Listen thoughtfully. Do not expect the leader to correct someone you think has a "wrong" answer. If you have a different opinion, express it graciously. Allow others to feel safe when offering their opinions.

3. Focus on the passage or topic being studied.

4. Do you tend to talk too much? Consider marking ahead of time the questions on which you wish to speak. If you are talking more than anyone else, use restraint. Every woman's voice is valuable; encourage others to speak up.

5. Do you seldom speak up? Offer input early in the discussion. Once you begin to participate, you will feel more comfortable. Your insights and experiences are valuable. Allow others to benefit from what only you can offer.

6. Are you here primarily for fellowship? Our need for community is important, so time for building relationships is built into the study. Engaging with God's Word is key for growing spiritually, and it is a fundamental part of this study. If you desire further connection with others, feel free to contact group members outside of class. Spend time doing fun things together.

7. Are you here primarily for Bible study? Just remember that spiritual growth happens in relationship with God and with each other. Other women would treasure your friendship and your encouragement. Time spent sharing life experiences, prayer requests, and praying together will enrich your life, too.

8. We want to create a safe environment where relationships are valued and everyone is comfortable expressing their hearts. So please, keep all personal contact information and sharing confidential. Please do not talk about politics or speak critically about other churches. Do not use the study for sales purposes.

9. Above all, have fun! Enjoy your growing relationships with God and with one another as you work through this study.

RUTH 1

Years ago, a popular television show caught national attention. On *This Is Your Life*, the host brought a lucky person on stage, and then her sisters, brothers, teachers, and coaches came forward to paint the picture of the contestant's life — when the person was born, how she grew up, who influenced her childhood, and much more flashed across the screen. Highs and lows . . . well, mostly the high points . . . delighted the studio audience. Every episode wrapped up with a happy ending; no exceptions.

But in truth, life doesn't always turn out the way we think it should, does it? Divorce, infertility, rejection, rehab, and loneliness seem to hover around every turn. We never expected life to be so hard.

Neither did the heroines of our Bible study, Naomi and Ruth. Life dealt them pain and suffering, loss and loneliness, uncertainty and jeopardy. How did they handle it? What can they teach us about living life well even when it's not the one we hoped to live? What role did God play in their lives . . . and what role does he continue to play in ours?

TRAGEDY STRIKES

In this first chapter of the book of Ruth, we enter an ancient world and meet two honest, courageous women who live out the truth that "life is hard *and* God is good."

"Life is hard and God is good."

Recommendation: Because the book of Ruth is a narrative, a story, you will understand it best if you read the whole story at once, from beginning to end. (You can do it! It's only four chapters.) Take time to do so right now. Then, as you approach each lesson, read the applicable chapter of Ruth before answering the questions.

1. Read Ruth 1:1–2. Then work through the map on the following page.

> *Note:* The names in these verses are tough to pronounce. So don't get caught up in reading them perfectly and forget to notice the action!

> In the days when the judges ruled, there was a famine in the land, and a man from Bethlehem in Judah, together with his wife and two sons, went to live for a while in the country of Moab. The man's name was Elimelech, his wife's name Naomi, and the names of his two sons were Mahlon and Kilion. They were Ephrathites from Bethlehem, Judah. And they went to Moab and lived there" (NIV).

When I come across a difficult word to pronounce, I just substitute "hard word" for it and keep going.

—Jackie

WHO do these verses seem to revolve around?

WHO is there? WHAT relationships exist?

WHEN did the story take place?

Use this map to retell what's happening. You can use words, draw pictures, or add X's to show the action in the passage.

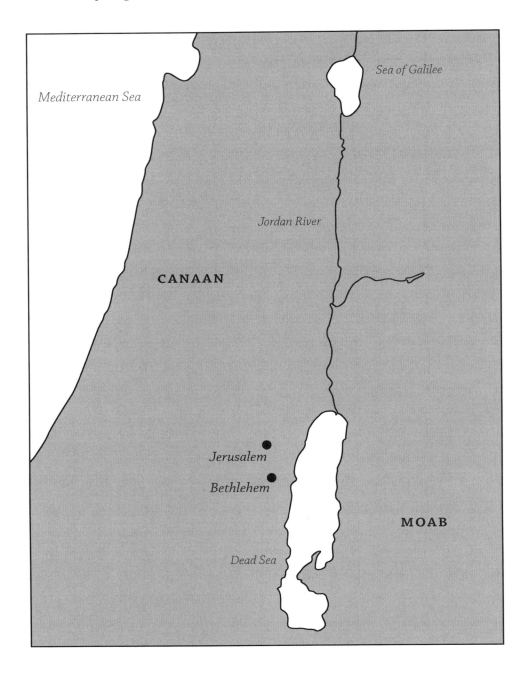

A BREAK FOR BACKGROUND

The era of the Judges was a dark time in Israel's history. After wandering in the desert of Sinai for forty years, God's people entered the land of Canaan, the land he had promised to Abraham. They were supposed to obey his commands and live a restful, peaceful life in this "promised land."

But they quickly forgot all the good things God had done for them, and we learn that the following generation "knew neither the Lord nor what he had done for Israel" (Judges 2:10, NIV). The nation went into an awful downward spiral as they habitually did "whatever they felt like doing" (Judges 17:6, MSG).

Because they abandoned God, they brought one trouble after another upon themselves in the form of invading armies, famine, and pestilence (see Deuteronomy 28:15, 22–24). The Israelites cried out to God for help. He provided a strong leader called a judge, who rescued them from the mess they created, and brought them back to him. Then the cycle started all over again.

Naomi and Ruth lived in the time of the Judges.

2. When you hear the term "refugee," what comes to mind? Perhaps you might describe a news story you have seen on television or read in the papers. Make a list of descriptive words, or draw a picture.

In the Old Testament, God forewarned the Israelites with very specific consequences to their disobedience. We do not see that repeated in the New Testament. Therefore, it would be inappropriate for Christians to attribute any type of tragedies, such as 9/11 or Hurricane Katrina, to God since God himself has not done so.

With that in mind, try to imagine Naomi's experience in Bethlehem (see Ruth 1:3–5). How do you think she must have felt? What obstacles, fears, limitations, feelings, hardships, and so on might she have faced?

3. Describe a time when you had to relocate or adjust to a new culture? What were the circumstances? What was the hardest part for you? How did you feel? What fears did you have?

4. Read Ruth 1:3–5 in The Message version below:

> Elimelech [*Eh-leh-meh-lek*] died and Naomi was left, she and her two sons. The sons took Moabite wives; the name of the first was Orpah [*Orr-puh*], the second Ruth. They lived there in Moab for the next ten years. But then the two brothers, Mahlon [*May-lahn*] and Kilion [*Kih-lee-ohn*], died. Now the woman was left without either her young men or her husband.

WHO are the participants mentioned? Who does the story seem to revolve around now?

WHERE are the people located?

WHEN is the action taking place? Are there any "time" words? WHAT are they?

WHAT is happening in these three verses? If you were to make a movie of these women, how would this particular chapter look like in the movie? What do the characters look like? Colors, body language, dialog, action, emotions, etc.?

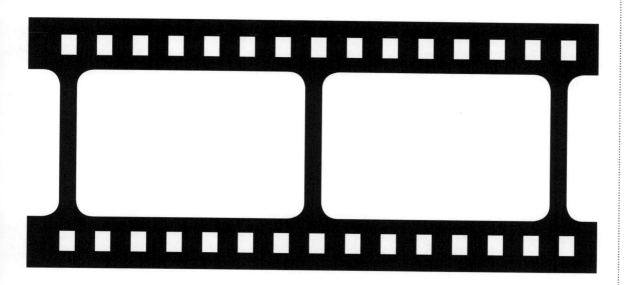

5. Reread Ruth 1:1–5. 5. List all of the losses that Naomi and Ruth experienced and brainstorm the lingering effects of each loss.

Primary Loss	Lingering Loss
loss of finances	loss of identity
loss of homeland	loss of community
loss of a spouse	

Now circle the one you identify with the most.

"In five short verses, death wipes the men off the scene, leaving three grieving widows behind. In a male-centered culture that ascribed value to women based on their relationships to men, these husbandless, sonless women hold no interest to anyone . Yet ironically, this is where the narrative heats up as the biblical spotlight settles on Naomi and an all-female cast." (Carolyn Custis James, 33)

Think through the loss you experienced. Describe the situation. Who did you share your experience with? How did she help you endure?

Did you keep your loss from anyone? Please explain your reasoning.

6. Read Ruth 1:6–13 aloud. Why did Naomi decide to go back to Bethlehem?

What name did Naomi use when she referred to God? What does this reveal about Naomi's heart toward God? (See 1:8–9, 19–21.)

Most of us have struggled with God like Naomi did. Please describe a situation like this from your personal life. If you had given God a name at that time, what name would it have been? What name would your friends have given you? Explain.

7. In 1:8–9, Naomi said to her two daughters-in-law, "Go back, each of you, to your mother's home. May the Lord show you kindness, as you have shown kindness (*hesed*) to your dead and to me. May the Lord grant that each of you will find rest in the home of another husband"(TNIV).

Look up the Hebrew word "hesed" in a concordance or online at discovertheword.org. List your findings here.

Note: "God's hesed is the centerpiece of the Ruth story, as it should be. The entire book zeros in on the weighty question of whether God's hesed has run out for Naomi. It's a question that sooner or later all of us will have to face for ourselves or for someone we love. And the story addresses this question, not by a spectacular vision or a divine voice speaking out of the heavens, but by God's people engaged in simple yet extraordinary acts of hesed." (Carolyn Custis James, 118)

8. According to Ruth 1:8–13, why did Naomi tell Orpah and Ruth to return home?

In verse 11, Naomi is alluding to the Israelite law which was given to protect the widow and guarantee that the *family name* would continue on. Deuteronomy 25:5 states, "If brothers are living together and one of them dies without a son, his widow must not marry outside the family. Her husband's brothers shall take her and marry her and fulfill the duty of a brother-in-law to her." Naomi was past child-bearing age and could no longer produce an heir to carry out that duty.

What did Orpah decide to do? Do you think this was the "sensible" thing to do? Why or why not?

What did each woman imagine awaited them in their respective futures?

Read verses 16–18. What do these verses reveal about Ruth and her decision?

Some scholars believe that this is the point where Ruth makes a deep commitment to Naomi's God, Yahweh.

9. Reread verses 16–18 below in both translations. Circle all the "you's." Put a square around the "I's." Write in the margins any observations, thoughts, or questions you have about Ruth.

> Don't urge me to leave you or to turn back from you. Where you go I will go, and where you stay I will stay. Your people will be my people and your God my God. Where you die I will die, and there I will be buried. May the LORD deal with me, be it ever so severely, if even death separates you and me.' When Naomi realized that Ruth was determined to go with her, she stopped urging her (NIV).

> But Ruth said, 'Don't force me to leave you; don't make me go home. Where you go, I go; and where you live, I'll live. Your people are my people, your God is my god; where you die, I'll die, and that's where I'll be buried, so help me God — not even death itself is going to come between us!' When Naomi saw that Ruth had her heart set on going with her, she gave in (MSG).

Think through the following statement. "Ruth clung to Naomi." That is the same language used in Genesis 2:24, when it says, "That is why a man leaves his father and mother and is united to his wife, and they become one flesh." Ruth's body language conveys her deep commitment to Naomi. And so do her words.

—Barb

DESPERATE HEARTACHE

Eugene Peterson described one of the reasons the Bible is so relatable to us even today: "No literature is more realistic and honest in facing the harsh facts of life than the Bible. At no time is there the faintest suggestion that the life of faith exempts us from difficulties . . . On every page of the Bible there is recognition that faith encounters troubles (42).

Ruth's vow of love and commitment must have brought great comfort to Naomi. However, it didn't take away the pain and grief Naomi must have felt.

10. Read the following verses aloud:

> So the two women went on until they came to Bethlehem. When they arrived in Bethlehem, the whole town was stirred because of them, and the women exclaimed, "Can this be Naomi?" "Don't call me Naomi," she told them. "Call me Mara, because the Almighty has made my life very bitter. I went away full, but the LORD has brought me back empty. Why call me Naomi? The LORD has afflicted me; the Almighty has brought misfortune upon me (1:19–21, NIV).

Why do you think the subject of God comes up more often when people are experiencing suffering, pain, or deep disappointment?

How do you feel about Naomi's strong words about God and his part in her suffering? Do you sense that she is right or wrong? In what ways do you respond mentally? Emotionally? Spiritually?

In Hebrew, Naomi means "pleasant," while Mara means "bitter."

Do you think it is important to be honest about how we feel — even about God — when deep, hard things happen? Why or why not? Are there any exceptions such as timing, audience, etc.? Please explain.

Naomi was not the only one to voice doubts and discouragement when life handed her pain. King David was honest with God about how he felt, too. He asked hard questions and opened up — as did Naomi — a dialogue with God that is real and authentic.

11. Read Psalm 13 reflectively (provided on the following page), taking your time and pondering each word. Circle the thoughts and/or questions you've asked in your times of pain and suffering.

PSALM 13

How long O Lord? Will you forget me forever? How long will you hide your face from me?

David's appeal to God

How long must I wrestle with my thoughts and every day have sorrow in my heart?

The cause of his pain

How long will my enemy triumph over me?

The request

Look on me and answer, O Lord my God. Give light to my eyes, or I will sleep in death;

The reason God should intervene

my enemy will say, "I have overcome him, and my foes will rejoice when I fall.

The confession of trust

But I trust in your unfailing love; my heart rejoices in your salvation.

The vow of praise

I will sing to the Lord, for he has been good to me." (NIV)

MY LAMENT

Maybe none of David's words mesh exactly with the hard question(s) you would like to ask God. If so, write out your question(s). Have you ever prayed, and asked God your questions? What's keeping you from sharing your heart with him?

David believed that God cared about his pain, so he voiced it. He processed his grief by pouring out his heart to God. He cried out to God, who not only allowed David to ask hard questions but was willing to wrestle through them with him.

12. To the right of Psalm 13 on page 22, David's lament (song of sorrow) has been broken down into segments as a pattern for you to follow. Write your own psalm of lament, using this model, or just pour out your heart to God about the disappointment and pain you've experienced in your life.

    You might also choose to pick a song that expresses your feelings. Write down the words. Do you have to change any of them? Or is it just right? If so, why?

    Take some time to envision saying or singing your psalm to Jesus.

RISING HOPE

The author of the book of Ruth ends this chapter of pain and suffering with hope: "So Naomi returned from Moab accompanied by Ruth the Moabitess, her daughter-in-law, arriving in Bethlehem as the barley harvest was beginning" (1:22, NIV).

The story has only just begun...

Lesson Two

RUTH 2

In the early nineties, Garth Brooks wrote a song about a man who is going on a date for the first time in years. The lyrics are his inner monologue, letting us in on his insecurity and fear. Although the song ends with hopeful anticipation, he doesn't let us forget the broken relationship that started it all. The last line of the song is the honest words of a weary traveler courageously choosing to journey on. He says, "This learning to live again is killing me."

Naomi and Ruth journeyed to Bethlehem to rebuild life from death . . . to learn to live again.

The book of Ruth opened at the lowest point of Ruth and Naomi's lives. Naomi lost her husband and her two sons, one of whom was Ruth's husband. Together, they were without income and identity in a difficult world. But in the midst of these terrible circumstances, Naomi and Ruth journeyed to Bethlehem to rebuild life from death . . . to learn to live again.

LEARNING TO LIVE AGAIN

Read Ruth 2 before you begin answering the questions in this lesson.

In the ancient world, survival was the primary objective and a male heir was needed to carry on the family name and help the family financially survive. Widows were either taken in by their husband's extended family, or they were expected to marry again. And if the woman was still of childbearing age, she was expected to marry her husband's brother and attempt to have a son, who would then inherit the estate of the widow's original husband.

Naomi and Ruth had no male relatives to provide for them. They were alone, helpless, hungry, and without means to care for themselves. Naomi was keenly aware she had little chance to remarry and conceive a son in her old age to provide for her or Ruth. On top of that, Ruth was a foreigner, a Moabite, with a history of barrenness.

Ruth's heritage and history of barrenness and Naomi's old age were all significant strikes against them when they entered Bethlehem.

"I'm gonna smile my best smile

And I'm gonna laugh like it's going out of style

Look into her eyes and pray that she don't see

That learning to live again is killing me."

—"Learning to Live Again," sung by Garth Brooks, written by Don Schiltz and Stephanie Davis, on The Chase Album, released 1992 on Liberty Records Album, produced by Allen Reynolds.

Barrenness was grounds for divorce in the ancient world and would have been looked down upon strongly by in-laws.

1. Imagine the contrast between Naomi and Ruth's life in Moab and what they experienced in Bethlehem. Why might it have been difficult for them to begin again? Fill out your answers below.

FROM MOAB TO BETHLEHEM

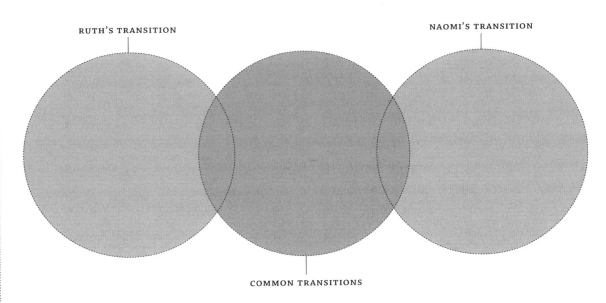

RUTH'S TRANSITION

NAOMI'S TRANSITION

COMMON TRANSITIONS

Think back to a difficult season you've walked through in your own life. In what ways did you have to "begin again"? Why was it difficult? What steps did you have to take to start over?

GOD PROVIDES FOR THOSE IN NEED

God's people lived with the assumption that God's hand is behind everything.

In this story, I keep thinking about God following me everywhere I go, and then when I sense he's there and look back, he quickly slips out of sight. I continue to move forward, and again I sense a presence, look, but I still don't see him although in reality, he's been there all along (Joshua 1:5).

—Jackie

2. Read Ruth 2:1–5, we are introduced to a new character: Boaz. What do we learn about him in verse one? Why is his relationship to Naomi important? (For a hint, look up Ruth 2 in a Bible commentary or two, Bible encyclopedia, or at www.bible.org.)

Note: This is where, in our minds, we typically think, "Here comes Boaz riding in on a white horse to save the day with romantic gestures." But the reality is more of what Carolyn Custis James says: "In this environment, for Boaz at least, Ruth was out of the running. Socially, a gleaner was lower than a field hand. Boaz was in a different social league from Ruth. Furthermore, this gleaner had a known history of barrenness, for her failure to deliver a son (or even a daughter for Mahlon) was no secret. Her qualifications would never match the search criteria of a man like Boaz" (Carolyn Custis James, 100).

3. Read Leviticus 19:1–2, 9–10. Write this passage in your own words.

   For whom was God concerned? How did he provide? Who else was involved?

   If you were a widow in ancient Israel, how would you feel about this law? Share your real emotions, good and bad. Be real.

4. Now read Ruth 2:2–3. Ruth chose to be faithful with the limited opportunities she had. Place yourself in Ruth's shoes and work through her decisions, thoughts, and emotions.

   What did Ruth decide to do?

   How did she take advantage of the limited opportunities before her?

   Do you think it was difficult for her to trust God?

   Do you think she trusted God's provision for her needs? Why or why not?

5. Work through each of the following verses, describing what each one tells you about God's heart for those in need.

Deuteronomy 10:18–19

Deuteronomy 15:7–11

Romans 8:26

2 Corinthians 1:4

OUR ROLE IN GOD'S PROVISION

6. Read the following quote:

> "Typically when harvesting a field, hired men went first — grasping handfuls of standing grain stalks with one hand, cutting them off at the base with a sickle, then laying the cut stalks on the ground. Female workers followed, gathering and binding cut grain into bundles to be carted to the threshing floor where raw kernels of grain were separated from the husks. Gleaners came last and were permitted in the field only after both teams of hired workers finished and bundled sheaves of grain were removed from the field" (Carolyn Custis James, 101).

Carefully view the scene of a typical harvest field. (Man harvester, woman bundler, gleaners, etc.)

Read Ruth's request in Ruth 2:5–7, and summarize it here. How did it fit within the "field culture"?

Based on this passage, put an "X" where you think Ruth is in the picture above.

Why do you think Ruth positioned herself there?

What does this reveal to you about her?

Gleaning is making a comeback in our generation to help feed the down-trodden. For information about modern gleaning visit www.endhunger.org.

7. Read Ruth 2 in the two translations provided. Circle all of the words in Ruth 2 that describe Ruth's character. Use them to write a short description of what she might have been like. Does she remind you of anyone you know?

Ruth 2 (NIV)

Now Naomi had a relative on her husband's side, from the clan of Elimelech, a man of standing, whose name was Boaz. And Ruth the Moabitess said to Naomi, "Let me go to the fields and pick up the leftover grain behind anyone in whose eyes I find favor." Naomi said to her, "Go ahead, my daughter." So she went out and began to glean in the fields behind the harvesters. As it turned out, she found herself working in a field belonging to Boaz, who was from the clan of Elimelech.

Just then Boaz arrived from Bethlehem and greeted the harvesters, "The LORD be with you!"

"The LORD bless you!" they called back.

Boaz asked the foreman of his harvesters, "Whose young woman is that?"

The foreman replied, "She is the Moabitess who came back from Moab with Naomi. She said, 'Please let me glean and gather among the sheaves behind the harvesters.' She went into the field and has worked steadily from morning till now, except for a short rest in the shelter." So Boaz said to Ruth, "My daughter, listen to me. Don't go and glean in another field and don't go away from here. Stay here with my servant girls. Watch the field where the men are harvesting, and follow along after the girls. I have told the men not to touch you. And whenever you are thirsty, go and get a drink from the water jars the men have filled."

At this, she bowed down with her face to the ground. She exclaimed, "Why have I found such favor in your eyes that you notice me—a foreigner?" Boaz replied, "I've been told all about what you have done for your mother-in-law since the death of your husband—how you left your father and mother and your homeland and came to live with a people you did not know before. May the LORD repay you for what you have done. May you be richly rewarded by the LORD, the God of Israel, under whose wings you have come to take refuge."

"May I continue to find favor in your eyes, my lord," she said. "You have given me comfort and have spoken kindly to your servant—though I do not have the standing of one of your servant girls." At mealtime Boaz said to her, "Come over here. Have some bread and dip it in the wine vinegar."

When she sat down with the harvesters, he offered her some roasted grain. She ate all she wanted and had some left over. As she got up to glean, Boaz gave orders to his men, "Even if she gathers among the sheaves, don't embarrass her. Rather, pull out some stalks for her from the bundles and leave them for her to pick up, and don't rebuke her."

So Ruth gleaned in the field until evening. Then she threshed the barley she had gathered, and it amounted to about an ephah. She carried it back to town, and her mother-in-law saw how much she had gathered. Ruth also brought out and gave her what she had left over after she had eaten enough.

Her mother-in-law asked her, "Where did you glean today? Where did you work? Blessed be the man who took notice of you!" Then Ruth told her mother-in-law about the one at whose place she had been working. "The name of the man I worked with today is Boaz," she said. "The LORD bless him!" Naomi said to her daughter-in-law. "He has not stopped showing his kindness to the living and the dead." She added, "That man is our close relative; he is one of our kinsman-redeemers." Then Ruth the Moabitess said, "He even said to me, 'Stay with my workers until they finish harvesting all my grain.'"

Naomi said to Ruth her daughter-in-law, "It will be good for you, my daughter, to go with his girls, because in someone else's field you might be harmed." So Ruth stayed close to the servant girls of Boaz to glean until the barley and wheat harvests were finished. And she lived with her mother-in-law.

Ruth 2 (MSG)

It so happened that Naomi had a relative by marriage, a man prominent and rich, connected with Elimelech's family. His name was Boaz. One day Ruth, the Moabite foreigner, said to Naomi, "I'm going to work; I'm going out to glean among the sheaves, following after some harvester who will treat me kindly." Naomi said, "Go ahead, dear daughter."

And so she set out. She went and started gleaning in a field, following in the wake of the harvesters. Eventually she ended up in the part of the field owned by Boaz, her father-in-law Elimelech's relative. A little later Boaz came out from Bethlehem, greeting his harvesters, "God be with you!" They replied, "And God bless you!" Boaz asked his young servant who was foreman over the farm hands, "Who is this young woman? Where did she come from?"

The foreman said, "Why, that's the Moabite girl, the one who came with Naomi from the country of Moab. She asked permission. 'Let me glean,' she said, 'and gather among the sheaves following after your harvesters.' She's been at it steady ever since, from early morning until now, without so much as a break."

Then Boaz spoke to Ruth: "Listen, my daughter. From now on don't go to any other field to glean — stay right here in this one. And stay close to my young women. Watch where they are harvesting and follow them. And don't worry about a thing; I've given orders to my servants not to harass you. When you get thirsty, feel free to go and drink from the water buckets that the servants have filled." She dropped to her knees, then bowed her face to the ground. "How does this happen that you should pick me out and treat me so kindly — *me*, a foreigner?"

Boaz answered her, "I've heard all about you — heard about the way you treated your mother-in-law after the death of her husband, and how you left your father and mother and the land of your birth and have come to live among a bunch of total strangers. God reward you well for what you've done — and with a generous bonus besides from God, to whom you've come seeking protection under his wings." She said, "Oh sir, such grace, such kindness — I don't deserve it. You've touched my heart, treated me like one of your own. And I don't even belong here!"

At the lunch break, Boaz said to her, "Come over here; eat some bread. Dip it in the wine." So she joined the harvesters. Boaz passed the roasted grain to her. She ate her fill and even had some left over. When she got up to go back to work, Boaz ordered his servants: "Let her glean where there's still plenty of grain on the ground — make it easy for her. Better yet, pull some of the good stuff out and leave it for her to glean. Give her special treatment."

Ruth gleaned in the field until evening. When she threshed out what she had gathered, she ended up with nearly a full sack of barley! She gathered up her gleanings, went back to town, and showed her mother-in-law the results of her day's work; she also gave her the leftovers from her lunch. Naomi asked her, "So where did you glean today? Whose field? God bless whoever it was who took such good care of you!" Ruth told her mother-in-law, "The man with whom I worked today? His name is Boaz."

Naomi said to her daughter-in-law, "Why, God bless that man! God hasn't quite walked out on us after all! He still loves us, in bad times as well as good!" Naomi went on, "That man, Ruth, is one of our circle of covenant redeemers, a close relative of ours!"

Ruth the Moabitess said, "Well, listen to this: He also told me, 'Stick with my workers until my harvesting is finished.'" Naomi said to Ruth, "That's wonderful, dear daughter! Do that! You'll be safe in the company of his young women; no danger now of being raped in some stranger's field." So Ruth did it — she stuck close to Boaz's young women, gleaning in the fields daily until both the barley and wheat harvesting were finished. And she continued living with her mother-in-law.

8. Reread Leviticus 19:9–10 below:

> When you reap the harvest of your land, do not reap to the very edges of your field or gather the gleanings of your harvest. Do not go over your vineyard a second time or pick up the grapes that have fallen. Leave them for the poor and the foreigner. I am the Lord your God (NIV).

Ruth's request pushed Boaz to be generous beyond what the law stipulated. What did Boaz do?

In Ruth 2:12, Boaz used a figure of speech called a *zoomorphism*, comparing an aspect of God to an animal, saying "under who's wings you have come to take refuge." Boaz is visually depicting God's protection of Ruth.

9. Drawing from what you know of Boaz in Ruth 2, write a character reference for Boaz.

Character Reference Form

Name:

Age:

Employment:

Country of residence:

	Excellent	Good	Poor	Don't Know
Communication skills				
Work quality				
Reliability				
Integrity				
Helpfulness				
Ability to work with others				
Leadership skills				
Additional comments:				

10. Boaz saw Ruth and Naomi's need, and he was in a position to meet that need and did so. Is there someone in your life whose need God has put you in a position to meet? Please describe the situation.

How could you meet that need? When? Be specific.

Share your action plan with someone else (face-to-face, email, phone, letter, Facebook, Twitter, etc.). Note: We are more likely to do something if we have shared it with another person.

11. What was Naomi's response to Ruth's choice to glean in Boaz's field? (See 2:20–22.) What specific name did she give him?

12. Read Deuteronomy 25:5–10, then carefully go through the quote below, and answer the questions on the on the following page.

> The 'nearest kinsman' or 'kinsman redeemer' is a *Goel*. The word means 'to redeem,' 'receive,' or 'buy back.' Provision was made in the Law of Moses for the poor person who was forced to sell part of his property or himself into slavery. His nearest of kin could step in and 'buy back' what his relative was forced to sell (Leviticus 25:48). The kinsman redeemer was a rich benefactor, or person who frees the debtor by paying the ransom price. 'If a fellow countryman of yours becomes so poor he has to sell part of his property, then his nearest kinsman is to come and buy back what his relative has sold' (Leviticus 25:25; cf. Ruth 4:4, 6). . . . If a family member died without an heir the kinsman gave his name by marrying the widow and rearing a son to hand down his name (Deuteronomy 25:5; Genesis 38:8; Ruth 3–4). (www.abideinchrist.com/messages/lev25v25.html).

The Levitical Law in Leviticus 25:25 redeemed the _____.

The Deuteronomical Law in Deuteronomy 25:5 redeemed the _____.

Who was required to redeem each of these back?

Did Boaz meet those requirements? Explain.

What do you think Naomi was "banking on" with Boaz?

Have you ever "banked on" someone before? When? What was the result?

We're now leaving the gleaning field and getting ready to head to the threshing floor . . .

Lesson Three

RUTH 3

The barley harvest in Bethlehem was a time of festivity and joy for all. After a long season of hard work and hope, Boaz and his workers rejoiced at the bringing in of grain. Meanwhile, Naomi and Ruth witnessed this community-wide celebration with the sober realization that their next meal was not guaranteed.

Without a man to care for them, they were still without identity and security. But God, in his loyal love, gave them a glimmer of hope through an encounter with Boaz, a close relative who had shown them great kindness. In this situation, Naomi had the choice to lay low and hope for the best or take a risk . . . boldly she led her daughter-in-law in a daring plan to secure a future and a hope.

LAYING IT ALL ON THE LINE

Read Ruth 3 before you begin to answer these questions.

1. Even if Boaz married Ruth, he was not required by Jewish Law to include Naomi in his new family. Considering what you know about Boaz's character from Ruth 2, how do you think that he would treat Naomi?

   According to Ruth 3:1–4, what plan did Naomi propose to Ruth?

   Do you think this was her intention from the beginning? (See Ruth 1:8.) Why or why not?

2. Do you tend to expect God to show up during a crisis or not? Place yourself on the continuum.

Always Expectant   *Rarely Expectant*

Fill in the sentence below to explain why.

I tend to expect/not expect God to show up because _____

_____

_____

_____

_____

Are there any exceptions? Please explain.

"By following Naomi's directions, Ruth will send nonverbal signals to Boaz that marriage is in view — a widow coming out of mourning, perfume in the air, the uncovering of a sleeping man's feet or legs, and her posture as a petitioner at his feet. Boaz will be in no doubt of what Ruth is proposing" (Carolyn Custis James, 146).

3. In the last chapter, we read Deuteronomy 25:5–10 and learned about God's provision for widows in ancient Israel. Do you think God's Law gave Naomi some confidence to instruct Ruth as she did? Please explain. Take a few moments to share your thoughts with your group.

Think through a time when you held onto one of God's promises from his Word. What happened? How did his promise encourage you, give you confidence, or comfort you?

If you are going through a difficult situation right now, take some time to find a Scripture passage that applies to your need. You might use a Bible concordance, do a keyword search on www.biblegateway.com, or ask a friend for a suggestion.

Then write the Scripture on a note card and place it in your purse or on your mirror. Ask the Lord to make it true in your life.

4. Read the passages below.

Exodus 34:6 provides one of the most complete descriptions of God's character in the Bible:

> The LORD passed in front of Moses, calling out, "Yahweh! The Lord! The God of compassion and mercy! I am slow to anger and filled with unfailing love (*hesed*) and faithfulness" (NLT).

Psalm 100:5 describes God like this,

> For the Lord is good and his love (*hesed*) endures forever; his faithfulness continues through all generations (NIV).

Think about what you have learned about the word "*hesed*," including the passages above. What thoughts come to mind about God's commitment to you during hard times?

 I remember learning Exodus 34:6 as the foundational verse describing God's character. I love that it teaches of God as long-suffering. To me, the image is one of locking arms and journeying together.

—Jackie

Think through a time you saw someone "lock arms" or show *hesed* with another in difficulty and walk the journey with her. (All the way; not a one-time pep talk.)

Was there a time you needed someone to walk beside you? Have you ever asked someone to walk alongside you with *hesed*?

What do we display when we show *hesed* to one another?

THE MOMENT OF TRUTH

"The threshing floor was a public place where animals trampled husks to separate out the grain. Workers would then toss the mixture into the air and let the wind carry away the chaff. Boaz stayed the night to guard his grain from thieves" (NIBC, 340).

5. Read Ruth 3:2–6. Imagine Ruth's arrival at the threshing floor. Describe the scene. Who's there? What does it smell like? What's the atmosphere? What is happening? Where's Ruth? (Google threshing floor images to get an idea of what this may have looked like.)

Dr. Ronald Allen says, "In uncovering his feet, Ruth would remove the edge of Boaz's outer garment from his feet and lie down by his uncovered feet. Touching and holding his feet was an act of submission. This was a daring and dramatic action that would call for a decision on his part to be her protector — and likely her husband" (Radmacher, et.al., 20).

Place yourself in Ruth's shoes. What might she have been feeling at this time? What about Naomi? (Remember God's provisions through the Law in Leviticus and Deuteronomy.)

Ruth trusted her mother-in-law, and followed her directions to wait for Boaz.

In Ruth 3:9, Ruth deliberately uses the same imagery Boaz uses in 2:12 to describe Ruth seeking the covering and protection of the Lord.

6. Read Ruth 3:4, 8–9. What did Naomi expect Ruth to ask Boaz? What exactly did Ruth say? What do you think her motivation might have been?

How do you feel about Ruth's bold request? Is this something you would have done? Why or why not?

GOD'S PROVISION; BOAZ'S PROTECTION

The provisions for widows in Jewish Law were very costly:

> "Since a father's estate was divided among his sons, when one son died childless, the surviving brother's inheritance automatically increased. The family pie was sliced into fewer (and therefore larger) pieces. According to Levirate Law, the brother whose duty it was to marry the widow was spoiling his own inheritance if he succeeded in fathering a son by her. The newborn would replace his deceased brother — and those lovely larger pieces of pie would shrink in size again because now there was one more heir to include in dividing family property.... The law wasn't simply a legal code, but a heart-piercing call to a higher way of living" (Carolyn Custis James, 150).

7. Answer the following about Boaz, according to Ruth 3:10–13. (Question continues on the following page.)

His response

His promise

The obstacle

With Boaz's wealth and prestige, it was highly likely Boaz was married (or widowed) with sons.

8. Some scholars believe the threshing floor was a place where prostitutes lingered. Underline, circle, or doodle your thoughts as to what in this passage may give some credence to this argument. Write any notes you like in the margins.

> "The Lord bless you, my daughter," he replied. "This kindness is greater than that which you showed earlier: You have not run after the younger men, whether rich or poor. And now, my daughter, don't be afraid. I will do for you all you ask. All the people of my town know that you are a woman of noble character. Although it is true that I am a guardian-redeemer of our family, there is another who is more closely related than I. Stay here for the night, and in the morning if he wants to do his duty as your guardian-redeemer, good; let him redeem you. But if he is not willing, as surely as the LORD lives I will do it. Lie here until morning." So she lay at his feet until morning, but got up before anyone could be recognized; and he said, "No one must know that a woman came to the threshing floor" (3:10–14, NIV).

Boaz instructs Ruth to lie down and sleep until morning. Boaz then sent Naomi a *seah* of grain, which scholars estimate ran anywhere from sixty to a hundred pounds (Carolyn Custis James, 154–5).

9. Consider how Naomi and Ruth felt (see question 5). How might Naomi and Ruth have felt after Boaz's response? How do you know? (Read 3:15–18.)

10. Using a dictionary and a Bible dictionary (you may find one online at www.biblegateway.org), write out several definitions of the word "hope." Then synthesize them into your own definition.

We also understand hope through our experiences. Think of a time in your life where you needed or found hope. Write out your experience as a narrative, composing a poem or song, making a collage, or drawing a picture. Share it with your group.

11. Proverbs 13:12 states, "Hope deferred makes the heart sick" (NIV). In the space provided, write why you think hope is so important during hard times.

Think of someone you know who's in a dark place. Reflect on the conversations you have had with her. Have you offered hope? If so, how? If not, how can you?

But the story isn't over yet ...

RUTH 4

Chapters 1 and 4 of the book of Ruth form a set of bookends that frame this dramatic story of loyal love and faithfulness. The biblical account begins with the death of a family and unbelievable heartache, continues by chronicling the rescue of that family, and finally points us to a beautiful, improbable future. Deep hope comes not just for Naomi and Ruth, but for all of us.

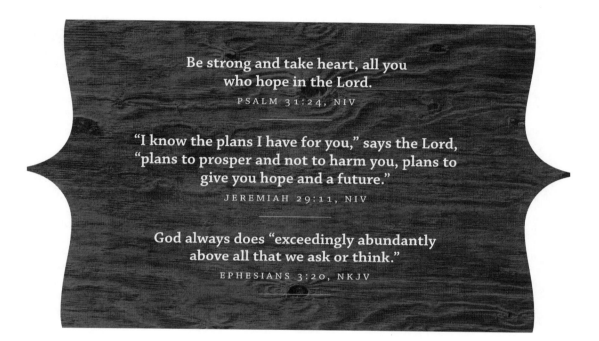

> Be strong and take heart, all you
> who hope in the Lord.
>
> PSALM 31:24, NIV

> "I know the plans I have for you," says the Lord,
> "plans to prosper and not to harm you, plans to
> give you hope and a future."
>
> JEREMIAH 29:11, NIV

> God always does "exceedingly abundantly
> above all that we ask or think."
>
> EPHESIANS 3:20, NKJV

A RESCUE OPERATION

Read chapter 4 before answering the following questions.

1. Reread Ruth 4:1–6 in the New Living Translation version on the following page. Underline the word "redeem" or any other form of that word used in the passage.

Boaz went to the town gate and took a seat there. Just then the family redeemer he had mentioned came by, so Boaz called out to him, "Come over here and sit down, friend. I want to talk to you." So they sat down together. Then Boaz called ten leaders from the town and asked them to sit as witnesses. And Boaz said to the family redeemer, "You know Naomi, who came back from Moab. She is selling the land that belonged to our relative Elimelech. I thought I should speak to you about it so that you can redeem it if you wish. If you want the land, then buy it here in the presence of these witnesses. But if you don't want it, let me know right away, because I am next in line to redeem it after you."

The man replied, "All right, I'll redeem it."

Then Boaz told him, "Of course, your purchase of the land from Naomi also requires that you marry Ruth, the Moabite widow. That way she can have children who will carry on her husband's name and keep the land in the family."

"Then I can't redeem it," the family redeemer replied, "because this might endanger my own estate. You redeem the land; I cannot do it."

Now look up the word *redeem* in a dictionary (dictionary.com) or in a bible dictionary (www.biblestudytools.com).

Define

Describe

Draw

2. Write one or two words beside each verse below to summarize what it teaches about God:

Exodus 3:7, 8

Psalm 19:14

Psalm 146:7

Isaiah 44:6

Write a sentence describing God's character as derived from these verses.

3. Chapter 4 uses the term "kinsman-redeemer" once again. Read Leviticus 25:23–27, 35. Why do you think God instituted the practice of redemption?

What does this reveal about his heart?

How does knowing this about God's character touch your heart or change your view of who he is or how you relate to him?

A RESCUE OPERATION

Boaz made a vow to become Ruth and Naomi's kinsman-redeemer . . . to reclaim the land that belonged to Elimelech and to marry Ruth as well (3:13).

4. Based on Ruth 3:12; 4:1–4, what obstacle did Boaz face?

Boaz knew his family situation — and thus the obstacle to marrying Ruth — prior to making his promise to her. Do you think he had a plan in mind for redeeming Ruth before visiting the village elders?

"The removal of a sandal was part of a legal transaction in ancient Israel (Deuteronomy 25:8–10). It would parallel the modern custom of concluding a transaction by signing a document or handing over a set of keys. By handing over his shoe, the close relative was symbolically handing over his right to walk on the land that was being sold" (Nelson Study Bible, 447).

5. Consider Ruth 4:5–6. At first the other relative agreed to act as Naomi's redeemer. Why did he eventually decline to do his duty? Summarize their arguments below.

Contrast the actions between Boaz and this man. What do their respective actions say about them?

Consider why this relative is never named. What thoughts, feelings, or questions come to mind?

Is there something in your life right now, or someone's close to you, where it's acceptable to follow the letter of the law, and be right, but perhaps God is calling you to something greater; to hesed love?

RESCUE, REDEMPTION, REJOICING

6. Take a look at Boaz's declaration in front of his community (see passage below). Circle any statement(s) which indicate that Boaz took action. Underline the word(s) that reveal Boaz had faith in God.

> Then Boaz said to the elders and to the crowd standing around, "You are witnesses that today I have bought from Naomi all the property of Elimelech, Kilion, and Mahlon. And with the land I have acquired Ruth, the Moabite widow of Mahlon, to be my wife. This way she can have a son to carry on the family name of her dead husband and to inherit the family property here in his hometown. You are all witnesses today" (Ruth 4:9, 10 NLT).

Carolyn Custis James makes this statement: "In an act of raw courage, [Ruth] persuades Boaz to join forces with her in rescuing Elimelech from the jaws of annihilation and Naomi from the grip of poverty and futility ... This is the Blessed Alliance — one of the strongest examples we see in the entire Old Testament of God's image bearers — male and female — serving God together" (Carolyn Custis James, 186–188).

According to Leviticus 25:25–27 and Deuteronomy 25:5, 7–10, a kinsman-redeemer must be qualified to fulfill the role. He must

- Be related by blood to those he redeems (kin),

- Be able to pay the price of redemption (have the resources)

- Be willing to redeem

According to Romans 3:23 and 6:16 and 20, we are in need of a redeemer. Jesus was related, able and willing to fulfill that role. He is our Redeemer. (See John 1:14, Hebrews 4:15, 2:14-15.)

7. Look up Ruth 2:1, 3:13. In your own words, describe how Boaz fulfilled all these qualifications.

Related

Able

Willing

8. What part did the community play in the redemptive process? (See Ruth 4:9-12.)

How did the community respond to Ruth and Boaz's redemptive actions?

Why do you think they responded that way?

Have you ever seen a community bring about a redemptive moment for someone? Please explain.

Is there someone you know who needs a redemptive moment? What would it look like? What would be your part? Who else would be involved? What might result? How can you make a move to bring about this redemptive moment for her this week?

Share your plan with someone else . . . maybe even enlist her help by letter, email, phone, Facebook, Twitter, face-to-face contact, etc.

9. Reread Ruth 1:19–22 and 4:13–17 below. Underline the contrast(s) between the two passages.

So the two of them continued on their journey. When they came to Bethlehem, the entire town was excited about their arrival. "Is it really Naomi?" the women asked. "Don't call me Naomi," she responded. "Instead, call me Mara, for the Almighty has made life very bitter for me. I went away full, but the LORD has brought me home empty. Why call me Naomi when the LORD has caused me to suffer and the Almighty has sent such tragedy upon me" (1:19–22, NLT).

So Boaz took Ruth into his home, and she became his wife. When he slept with her, the Lord enabled her to become pregnant, and she gave birth to a son. Then the women of the town said to Naomi, "Praise the Lord, who has now provided a redeemer for your family! May this child be famous in Israel. May he restore your youth and care for you in your old age. For he is the son of your daughter-in-law who loves you and has been better to you than seven sons!" Naomi took the baby and cuddled him to her breast. And she cared for him as if he were her own. The neighbor women said, "Now at last Naomi has a son again!" And they named him Obed. He became the father of Jesse and the grandfather of David (4:13–17, NLT).

Now think through the ways God's plan of redemption changed Naomi, Ruth, and Boaz's lives. List as many as you can below, then share your list with your group and make it as complete as possible.

THE EFFECTS OF REDEMPTION		
Naomi	**Ruth**	**Boaz**

10. Pretend you are Naomi. Write a short family newsletter updating friends about the big news (see following page).

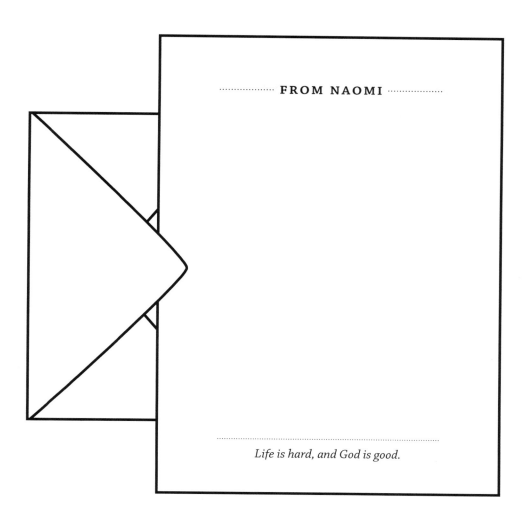

FROM NAOMI

....

Life is hard, and God is good.

A HOPE AND A FUTURE

11. Compare Ruth 4:18–22 to the genealogy in Matthew 1:1–6, 16. Why do you think God chose to include Boaz and Ruth in Jesus' lineage? What does this reveal about God's heart?

12. Think through the scope of Christ's redemption. Imagine Naomi, Ruth, and Boaz looking into Obed's little face after his birth. What might they have thought about God? His provision?

"The story concludes with David's genealogy, beginning with Perez, the son of Judah and Tamar. The genealogy of David is not really an appendix, but an essential element demonstrating the author's purpose — and the purpose of the Lord in the building of the family line of King David and the Messiah" (Nelson Study Bible, 448).

Take a minute to consider if it is possible that God's provision in our lives today could impact generations to come. Write your thoughts.

13. Life isn't always wrapped up in a pretty bow. Not everyone's story has a "happily ever after" ending. How would you speak hope into a woman's life that doesn't have a "happily ever after"?

Chapter 1 ended in a psalm of lament. Look back at the one you wrote. Tragedy and heartache filled the landscape with only whispers of hope blowing in the breeze. But chapter 4 ends with great cause for gratitude and praise, not just for Ruth and Naomi, but for us all, because our Redeemer lives!

14. Write a psalm of praise about a hardship for which you have come through and are now resting on the other side. Or, if you are in the middle of a hard time, try writing a psalm of hope for the future when you will be on the other side.

Here is an example of a psalm of praise: To the right of Psalm 100, three segments have been labeled as a possible pattern for you to follow. You may want to use this pattern, but please don't let it box you in.

PSALM 100

MY PRAISE

Shout for joy to the LORD, all the earth, Worship the LORD with gladness; Come before him with joyful songs.

Call to Praise

Know the LORD is God. It is he who made us, and we are his, We are his people, the sheep of his pasture.

Reason for praise

Enter his gates with thanksgiving and his courts with praise, Give thanks to him and praise his name. For the LORD is good and his love endures forever;his faithfulness continues throughall generations. (NIV)

Renewed call to praise

For the Lord is good and his love endures forever;
his faithfulness continues through all generations.
Psalm 100:5, NIV

BIBLIOGRAPHY

Constable, Dr. Thomas. "Notes on Ruth" Sonic Light: Tyndale Seminary Press, 2010.

Hybels, Lynn. *Nice Girls Don't Change the World*. Grand Rapids, Mich.: Zondervan, 2005.

James, Carolyn Custis. *The Gospel of Ruth*, Grand Rapids, Mich. Zondervan, 2008.

Nelson, Thomas. *The Nelson Study Bible*. Thomas Nelson, Inc., 1997.

Peterson, Eugene H. *A Long Obedience in the Same Direction: Discipleship in an Instant Society*. Downers Grove, Ill.: InterVarsity Press, 2000.

Radmacher, Earl D., Ronald B. Allen, and H. Wayne. House. *Nelson's New Illustrated Bible Commentary*. Nashville: Thomas Nelson, 1999.

"Ruth, Theology of," *Baker's Evangelical Dictionary of Biblical Theology Online*. www.biblestudytools.com/dictionaries/bakers-evangelical-dictionary/ruth-theology-of.html. Accessed June 30, 2011.

Winner, Lauren. *Mudhouse Sabbath*. Brewster, Mass.: Paraclete Press, 2007.

Websites

www.biblestudytools.com

www.biblegateway.com

18113303R00035

Made in the USA
San Bernardino, CA
30 December 2014

THIS LOG BOOK BELONGS TO :

Name : ....

Phone : ....

Adresse : ....

Aquarium Freshwater Parameters

Element	Ideal Level	Testing Frequency & Instructions
Temperature	72 - 82 °F 22 - 28 °C	<u>Daily</u> : Make sure your tank's water temperature tests every day
pH	6.5 - 8.5	<u>Weekly</u> : PH is very important in maintaining healthy fish, since high or low pH levels can stress fish and threaten their overall health
Ammonia	0 ppm	<u>Weekly</u> : Ammonia is highly toxic to fish, and can kill them rapidly
Nitrite	0 ppm	<u>Weekly</u> : Nitrite reduces the oxygen content in the blood of your fish.
Nitrate	0 - 40 ppm	<u>Weekly</u> : Changing the water should help lower the nitrate levels
Magnesium	1200 - 1350 ppm	<u>Weekly</u> : It is better to keep Magnesium level right at 1350
Alkalinity (Carbonate Hardness)	7 - 12 dKH 120 - 220 ppm	<u>Weekly</u> : It's a measure of how good the water quality is
Phosphates	0 ppm	<u>Weekly tracking</u>
Calcium	400 - 450 ppm	<u>Weekly</u> : Check regularly and change the supplement by dosing if possible
Water Change	<u>Weekly</u> : Replace 10 - 15% of the tank with clean water <u>Monthly</u> : Replace 20 - 25% of the tank with clean water	

Aquarium Equipment Replacement

Equipment	Lifespan
Filter Foams	4 – 6 weeks
UV Bulbs	6 – 12 months
Filter O-Rings	Once there are some signs of damage
Filter Impellers	Once there are some signs of damage
Filter Pumps	Pumps only require replacement if they are defective
Heater	Once there are some signs of damage
Pump	Duration varies depending on Pump Type

Tank : .... Date : ....

Fish Count : .... Feeding : ....

FRESHWATER PARAMETERS

Water Temperature :	Nitrate Level :
pH Level :	Magnesium :
Ammonia :	Alkalinity : (Carbonate Hardness)
Nitrite Level :	Phosphates :
Calcium Level :	Water Change 10 - 15 % of water / 20 - 25 % of water
Salinity Level :	Other Condition :

TANK EQUIPMENT CHECK

COMPONENT	STATUS	CLEANING DATE	REPLACEMENT DATE	OBSERVATIONS
Filters :				
Pumps :				
Heaters :				
Lighting :				
Aquarium Walls				
Other Component				

NOTES : ....

....

....

....

Tank : .... Date : ....
Fish Count : .... Feeding : ....

FRESHWATER PARAMETERS

Water Temperature :	Nitrate Level :
pH Level :	Magnesium :
Ammonia :	Alkalinity : (Carbonate Hardness)
Nitrite Level :	Phosphates :
Calcium Level :	Water Change — 10 - 15 % of water / 20 - 25 % of water
Salinity Level :	Other Condition :

TANK EQUIPMENT CHECK

COMPONENT	STATUS	CLEANING DATE	REPLACEMENT DATE	OBSERVATIONS
Filters :				
Pumps :				
Heaters :				
Lighting :				
Aquarium Walls				
Other Component				

NOTES : ....

....

....

....

Tank : .... Date : ....

Fish Count : .... Feeding : ....

FRESHWATER PARAMETERS

Water Temperature :	Nitrate Level :
pH Level :	Magnesium :
Ammonia :	Alkalinity : (Carbonate Hardness)
Nitrite Level :	Phosphates :
Calcium Level :	Water Change — 10 - 15 % of water — 20 - 25 % of water —
Salinity Level :	Other Condition :

TANK EQUIPMENT CHECK

COMPONENT	STATUS	CLEANING DATE	REPLACEMENT DATE	OBSERVATIONS
Filters :				
Pumps :				
Heaters :				
Lighting :				
Aquarium Walls				
Other Component				

NOTES : ....

....

....

....

Tank : .... Date : ....

Fish Count : .... Feeding : ....

FRESHWATER PARAMETERS

Water Temperature :	Nitrate Level :
pH Level :	Magnesium :
Ammonia :	Alkalinity : (Carbonate Hardness)
Nitrite Level :	Phosphates :
Calcium Level :	Water Change — 10 - 15 % of water / 20 - 25 % of water
Salinity Level :	Other Condition :

TANK EQUIPMENT CHECK

COMPONENT	STATUS	CLEANING DATE	REPLACEMENT DATE	OBSERVATIONS
Filters :				
Pumps :				
Heaters :				
Lighting :				
Aquarium Walls				
Other Component				

NOTES : ....

....

....

....

Tank : .... Date : ....

Fish Count : .... Feeding : ....

FRESHWATER PARAMETERS

Water Temperature :	Nitrate Level :
pH Level :	Magnesium :
Ammonia :	Alkalinity : (Carbonate Hardness)
Nitrite Level :	Phosphates :
Calcium Level :	Water Change 10 - 15 % of water / 20 - 25 % of water
Salinity Level :	Other Condition :

TANK EQUIPMENT CHECK

COMPONENT	STATUS	CLEANING DATE	REPLACEMENT DATE	OBSERVATIONS
Filters :				
Pumps :				
Heaters :				
Lighting :				
Aquarium Walls				
Other Component				

NOTES : ....

....

....

....

Tank : .... Date : ....

Fish Count : .... Feeding : ....

FRESHWATER PARAMETERS

Water Temperature :	Nitrate Level :
pH Level :	Magnesium :
Ammonia :	Alkalinity : (Carbonate Hardness)
Nitrite Level :	Phosphates :
Calcium Level :	Water Change — 10 - 15 % of water / 20 - 25 % of water
Salinity Level :	Other Condition :

TANK EQUIPMENT CHECK

COMPONENT	STATUS	CLEANING DATE	REPLACEMENT DATE	OBSERVATIONS
Filters :				
Pumps :				
Heaters :				
Lighting :				
Aquarium Walls				
Other Component				

NOTES : ....

....

....

....

Tank : .... Date : ....

Fish Count : .... Feeding : ....

FRESHWATER PARAMETERS

Water Temperature :	Nitrate Level :
pH Level :	Magnesium :
Ammonia :	Alkalinity : (Carbonate Hardness)
Nitrite Level :	Phosphates :
Calcium Level :	Water Change / 10 - 15 % of water / 20 - 25 % of water
Salinity Level :	Other Condition :

TANK EQUIPMENT CHECK

COMPONENT	STATUS	CLEANING DATE	REPLACEMENT DATE	OBSERVATIONS
Filters :				
Pumps :				
Heaters :				
Lighting :				
Aquarium Walls				
Other Component				

NOTES : ....

....

....

....

Tank : .... Date : ....

Fish Count : .... Feeding : ....

FRESHWATER PARAMETERS

Water Temperature :	Nitrate Level :
pH Level :	Magnesium :
Ammonia :	Alkalinity : (Carbonate Hardness)
Nitrite Level :	Phosphates :
Calcium Level :	Water Change — 10 - 15 % of water / 20 - 25 % of water
Salinity Level :	Other Condition :

TANK EQUIPMENT CHECK

COMPONENT	STATUS	CLEANING DATE	REPLACEMENT DATE	OBSERVATIONS
Filters :				
Pumps :				
Heaters :				
Lighting :				
Aquarium Walls				
Other Component				

NOTES : ....

....

....

....

Tank : ....   Date : ....

Fish Count : ....   Feeding : ....

FRESHWATER PARAMETERS

Water Temperature :	Nitrate Level :
pH Level :	Magnesium :
Ammonia :	Alkalinity : (Carbonate Hardness)
Nitrite Level :	Phosphates :
Calcium Level :	Water Change — 10 - 15 % of water / 20 - 25 % of water
Salinity Level :	Other Condition :

TANK EQUIPMENT CHECK

COMPONENT	STATUS	CLEANING DATE	REPLACEMENT DATE	OBSERVATIONS
Filters :				
Pumps :				
Heaters :				
Lighting :				
Aquarium Walls				
Other Component				

NOTES : ....

....

....

....

Tank : .... Date : ....
Fish Count : .... Feeding : ....

FRESHWATER PARAMETERS

Water Temperature :	Nitrate Level :
pH Level :	Magnesium :
Ammonia :	Alkalinity : (Carbonate Hardness)
Nitrite Level :	Phosphates :
Calcium Level :	Water Change — 10 - 15 % of water / 20 - 25 % of water
Salinity Level :	Other Condition :

TANK EQUIPMENT CHECK

COMPONENT	STATUS	CLEANING DATE	REPLACEMENT DATE	OBSERVATIONS
Filters :				
Pumps :				
Heaters :				
Lighting :				
Aquarium Walls				
Other Component				

NOTES : ....
....
....
....

Tank : .... Date : ....

Fish Count : .... Feeding : ....

FRESHWATER PARAMETERS

Water Temperature :	Nitrate Level :
pH Level :	Magnesium :
Ammonia :	Alkalinity : (Carbonate Hardness)
Nitrite Level :	Phosphates :
Calcium Level :	Water Change — 10 - 15 % of water / 20 - 25 % of water
Salinity Level :	Other Condition :

TANK EQUIPMENT CHECK

COMPONENT	STATUS	CLEANING DATE	REPLACEMENT DATE	OBSERVATIONS
Filters :				
Pumps :				
Heaters :				
Lighting :				
Aquarium Walls				
Other Component				

NOTES : ....

....

....

....

Tank : .... Date : ....

Fish Count : .... Feeding : ....

FRESHWATER PARAMETERS

Water Temperature :	Nitrate Level :
pH Level :	Magnesium :
Ammonia :	Alkalinity : (Carbonate Hardness)
Nitrite Level :	Phosphates :
Calcium Level :	Water Change — 10 - 15 % of water / 20 - 25 % of water
Salinity Level :	Other Condition :

TANK EQUIPMENT CHECK

COMPONENT	STATUS	CLEANING DATE	REPLACEMENT DATE	OBSERVATIONS
Filters :				
Pumps :				
Heaters :				
Lighting :				
Aquarium Walls				
Other Component				

NOTES : ....

....

....

....

Tank : .... Date : ....

Fish Count : .... Feeding : ....

FRESHWATER PARAMETERS

Water Temperature :	Nitrate Level :
pH Level :	Magnesium :
Ammonia :	Alkalinity : (Carbonate Hardness)
Nitrite Level :	Phosphates :
Calcium Level :	Water Change — 10 - 15 % of water / 20 - 25 % of water
Salinity Level :	Other Condition :

TANK EQUIPMENT CHECK

COMPONENT	STATUS	CLEANING DATE	REPLACEMENT DATE	OBSERVATIONS
Filters :				
Pumps :				
Heaters :				
Lighting :				
Aquarium Walls				
Other Component				

NOTES : ....

....

....

....

Tank : .... Date : ....

Fish Count : .... Feeding : ....

FRESHWATER PARAMETERS

Water Temperature :	Nitrate Level :
pH Level :	Magnesium :
Ammonia :	Alkalinity : (Carbonate Hardness)
Nitrite Level :	Phosphates :
Calcium Level :	Water Change — 10 - 15 % of water 20 - 25 % of water
Salinity Level :	Other Condition :

TANK EQUIPMENT CHECK

COMPONENT	STATUS	CLEANING DATE	REPLACEMENT DATE	OBSERVATIONS
Filters :				
Pumps :				
Heaters :				
Lighting :				
Aquarium Walls				
Other Component				

NOTES : ....

....

....

....

Tank : .... Date : ....

Fish Count : .... Feeding : ....

FRESHWATER PARAMETERS

Water Temperature :	Nitrate Level :
pH Level :	Magnesium :
Ammonia :	Alkalinity : (Carbonate Hardness)
Nitrite Level :	Phosphates :
Calcium Level :	Water Change — 10 - 15 % of water / 20 - 25 % of water
Salinity Level :	Other Condition :

TANK EQUIPMENT CHECK

COMPONENT	STATUS	CLEANING DATE	REPLACEMENT DATE	OBSERVATIONS
Filters :				
Pumps :				
Heaters :				
Lighting :				
Aquarium Walls				
Other Component				

NOTES : ....

....

....

....

Tank : ....   Date : ....

Fish Count : ....   Feeding : ....

FRESHWATER PARAMETERS

Water Temperature :	Nitrate Level :
pH Level :	Magnesium :
Ammonia :	Alkalinity : (Carbonate Hardness)
Nitrite Level :	Phosphates :
Calcium Level :	Water Change — 10 - 15 % of water / 20 - 25 % of water
Salinity Level :	Other Condition :

TANK EQUIPMENT CHECK

COMPONENT	STATUS	CLEANING DATE	REPLACEMENT DATE	OBSERVATIONS
Filters :				
Pumps :				
Heaters :				
Lighting :				
Aquarium Walls				
Other Component				

NOTES : ....

....

....

....

Tank : .... Date : ....

Fish Count : .... Feeding : ....

FRESHWATER PARAMETERS

Water Temperature :	Nitrate Level :
pH Level :	Magnesium :
Ammonia :	Alkalinity : (Carbonate Hardness)
Nitrite Level :	Phosphates :
Calcium Level :	Water Change 10 - 15 % of water
	20 - 25 % of water
Salinity Level :	Other Condition :

TANK EQUIPMENT CHECK

COMPONENT	STATUS	CLEANING DATE	REPLACEMENT DATE	OBSERVATIONS
Filters :				
Pumps :				
Heaters :				
Lighting :				
Aquarium Walls				
Other Component				

NOTES : ....

....

....

....

Tank : .... Date : ....

Fish Count : .... Feeding : ....

FRESHWATER PARAMETERS

Water Temperature :	Nitrate Level :
pH Level :	Magnesium :
Ammonia :	Alkalinity : (Carbonate Hardness)
Nitrite Level :	Phosphates :
Calcium Level :	Water Change — 10 - 15 % of water / 20 - 25 % of water
Salinity Level :	Other Condition :

TANK EQUIPMENT CHECK

COMPONENT	STATUS	CLEANING DATE	REPLACEMENT DATE	OBSERVATIONS
Filters :				
Pumps :				
Heaters :				
Lighting :				
Aquarium Walls				
Other Component				

NOTES : ....

....

....

....

Tank : ....   Date : ....

Fish Count : ....   Feeding : ....

FRESHWATER PARAMETERS

Water Temperature :	Nitrate Level :
pH Level :	Magnesium :
Ammonia :	Alkalinity : (Carbonate Hardness)
Nitrite Level :	Phosphates :
Calcium Level :	Water Change — 10 - 15 % of water / 20 - 25 % of water
Salinity Level :	Other Condition :

TANK EQUIPMENT CHECK

COMPONENT	STATUS	CLEANING DATE	REPLACEMENT DATE	OBSERVATIONS
Filters :				
Pumps :				
Heaters :				
Lighting :				
Aquarium Walls				
Other Component				

NOTES : ....

....

....

....

Tank : .... Date : ....
Fish Count : .... Feeding : ....

FRESHWATER PARAMETERS

Water Temperature :	Nitrate Level :
pH Level :	Magnesium :
Ammonia :	Alkalinity : (Carbonate Hardness)
Nitrite Level :	Phosphates :
Calcium Level :	Water Change — 10 - 15 % of water 20 - 25 % of water
Salinity Level :	Other Condition :

TANK EQUIPMENT CHECK

COMPONENT	STATUS	CLEANING DATE	REPLACEMENT DATE	OBSERVATIONS
Filters :				
Pumps :				
Heaters :				
Lighting :				
Aquarium Walls				
Other Component				

NOTES : ....
....
....
....

Tank : .... Date : ....

Fish Count : .... Feeding : ....

FRESHWATER PARAMETERS

Water Temperature :	Nitrate Level :
pH Level :	Magnesium :
Ammonia :	Alkalinity : (Carbonate Hardness)
Nitrite Level :	Phosphates :
Calcium Level :	Water Change — 10 - 15 % of water / 20 - 25 % of water
Salinity Level :	Other Condition :

TANK EQUIPMENT CHECK

COMPONENT	STATUS	CLEANING DATE	REPLACEMENT DATE	OBSERVATIONS
Filters :				
Pumps :				
Heaters :				
Lighting :				
Aquarium Walls				
Other Component				

NOTES : ....

....

....

....

Tank : ....   Date : ....

Fish Count : ....   Feeding : ....

FRESHWATER PARAMETERS

Water Temperature :	Nitrate Level :
pH Level :	Magnesium :
Ammonia :	Alkalinity : (Carbonate Hardness)
Nitrite Level :	Phosphates :
Calcium Level :	Water Change — 10 - 15 % of water / 20 - 25 % of water
Salinity Level :	Other Condition :

TANK EQUIPMENT CHECK

COMPONENT	STATUS	CLEANING DATE	REPLACEMENT DATE	OBSERVATIONS
Filters :				
Pumps :				
Heaters :				
Lighting :				
Aquarium Walls				
Other Component				

NOTES : ....

....

....

....

Tank : ....   Date : ....

Fish Count : ....   Feeding : ....

FRESHWATER PARAMETERS

Water Temperature :	Nitrate Level :
pH Level :	Magnesium :
Ammonia :	Alkalinity : (Carbonate Hardness)
Nitrite Level :	Phosphates :
Calcium Level :	Water Change — 10 - 15 % of water / 20 - 25 % of water
Salinity Level :	Other Condition :

TANK EQUIPMENT CHECK

COMPONENT	STATUS	CLEANING DATE	REPLACEMENT DATE	OBSERVATIONS
Filters :				
Pumps :				
Heaters :				
Lighting :				
Aquarium Walls				
Other Component				

NOTES : ....

....

....

....

Tank : .... Date : ....

Fish Count : .... Feeding : ....

FRESHWATER PARAMETERS

Water Temperature :	Nitrate Level :
pH Level :	Magnesium :
Ammonia :	Alkalinity : (Carbonate Hardness)
Nitrite Level :	Phosphates :
Calcium Level :	Water Change — 10 - 15 % of water / 20 - 25 % of water
Salinity Level :	Other Condition :

TANK EQUIPMENT CHECK

COMPONENT	STATUS	CLEANING DATE	REPLACEMENT DATE	OBSERVATIONS
Filters :				
Pumps :				
Heaters :				
Lighting :				
Aquarium Walls				
Other Component				

NOTES : ....
....
....
....

Tank : ....   Date : ....

Fish Count : ....   Feeding : ....

FRESHWATER PARAMETERS

Water Temperature :	Nitrate Level :
pH Level :	Magnesium :
Ammonia :	Alkalinity : (Carbonate Hardness)
Nitrite Level :	Phosphates :
Calcium Level :	Water Change — 10 - 15 % of water / 20 - 25 % of water
Salinity Level :	Other Condition :

TANK EQUIPMENT CHECK

COMPONENT	STATUS	CLEANING DATE	REPLACEMENT DATE	OBSERVATIONS
Filters :				
Pumps :				
Heaters :				
Lighting :				
Aquarium Walls				
Other Component				

NOTES : ....

....

....

....

Tank : .... Date : ....

Fish Count : .... Feeding : ....

FRESHWATER PARAMETERS

Water Temperature :	Nitrate Level :
pH Level :	Magnesium :
Ammonia :	Alkalinity : (Carbonate Hardness)
Nitrite Level :	Phosphates :
Calcium Level :	Water Change — 10 - 15 % of water / 20 - 25 % of water
Salinity Level :	Other Condition :

TANK EQUIPMENT CHECK

COMPONENT	STATUS	CLEANING DATE	REPLACEMENT DATE	OBSERVATIONS
Filters :				
Pumps :				
Heaters :				
Lighting :				
Aquarium Walls				
Other Component				

NOTES : ....

....

....

....

Tank : .... Date : ....

Fish Count : .... Feeding : ....

FRESHWATER PARAMETERS

Water Temperature :	Nitrate Level :
pH Level :	Magnesium :
Ammonia :	Alkalinity : (Carbonate Hardness)
Nitrite Level :	Phosphates :
Calcium Level :	Water Change — 10 - 15 % of water / 20 - 25 % of water
Salinity Level :	Other Condition :

TANK EQUIPMENT CHECK

COMPONENT	STATUS	CLEANING DATE	REPLACEMENT DATE	OBSERVATIONS
Filters :				
Pumps :				
Heaters :				
Lighting :				
Aquarium Walls				
Other Component				

NOTES : ....

....

....

....

Tank : .... Date : ....

Fish Count : .... Feeding : ....

FRESHWATER PARAMETERS

Water Temperature :	Nitrate Level :
pH Level :	Magnesium :
Ammonia :	Alkalinity : (Carbonate Hardness)
Nitrite Level :	Phosphates :
Calcium Level :	Water Change — 10 - 15 % of water / 20 - 25 % of water
Salinity Level :	Other Condition :

TANK EQUIPMENT CHECK

COMPONENT	STATUS	CLEANING DATE	REPLACEMENT DATE	OBSERVATIONS
Filters :				
Pumps :				
Heaters :				
Lighting :				
Aquarium Walls				
Other Component				

NOTES : ....

....

....

....

Tank : .... Date : ....

Fish Count : .... Feeding : ....

FRESHWATER PARAMETERS

Water Temperature :	Nitrate Level :
pH Level :	Magnesium :
Ammonia :	Alkalinity : (Carbonate Hardness)
Nitrite Level :	Phosphates :
Calcium Level :	Water Change — 10 - 15 % of water / 20 - 25 % of water
Salinity Level :	Other Condition :

TANK EQUIPMENT CHECK

COMPONENT	STATUS	CLEANING DATE	REPLACEMENT DATE	OBSERVATIONS
Filters :				
Pumps :				
Heaters :				
Lighting :				
Aquarium Walls				
Other Component				

NOTES : ....

....

....

....

Tank : .... Date : ....

Fish Count : .... Feeding : ....

FRESHWATER PARAMETERS

Water Temperature :	Nitrate Level :
pH Level :	Magnesium :
Ammonia :	Alkalinity : (Carbonate Hardness)
Nitrite Level :	Phosphates :
Calcium Level :	Water Change — 10 - 15 % of water 20 - 25 % of water
Salinity Level :	Other Condition :

TANK EQUIPMENT CHECK

COMPONENT	STATUS	CLEANING DATE	REPLACEMENT DATE	OBSERVATIONS
Filters :				
Pumps :				
Heaters :				
Lighting :				
Aquarium Walls				
Other Component				

NOTES : ....

....

....

....

Tank : ....   Date : ....

Fish Count : ....   Feeding : ....

FRESHWATER PARAMETERS

Water Temperature :	Nitrate Level :
pH Level :	Magnesium :
Ammonia :	Alkalinity : (Carbonate Hardness)
Nitrite Level :	Phosphates :
Calcium Level :	Water Change — 10 - 15 % of water / 20 - 25 % of water
Salinity Level :	Other Condition :

TANK EQUIPMENT CHECK

COMPONENT	STATUS	CLEANING DATE	REPLACEMENT DATE	OBSERVATIONS
Filters :				
Pumps :				
Heaters :				
Lighting :				
Aquarium Walls				
Other Component				

NOTES : ....

....

....

....

Tank : .... Date : ....

Fish Count : .... Feeding : ....

FRESHWATER PARAMETERS

Water Temperature :	Nitrate Level :
pH Level :	Magnesium :
Ammonia :	Alkalinity : (Carbonate Hardness)
Nitrite Level :	Phosphates :
Calcium Level :	Water Change — 10 - 15 % of water / 20 - 25 % of water
Salinity Level :	Other Condition :

TANK EQUIPMENT CHECK

COMPONENT	STATUS	CLEANING DATE	REPLACEMENT DATE	OBSERVATIONS
Filters :				
Pumps :				
Heaters :				
Lighting :				
Aquarium Walls				
Other Component				

NOTES : ....

....

....

....

Tank : ....   Date : ....

Fish Count : ....   Feeding : ....

FRESHWATER PARAMETERS

Water Temperature :	Nitrate Level :
pH Level :	Magnesium :
Ammonia :	Alkalinity : (Carbonate Hardness)
Nitrite Level :	Phosphates :
Calcium Level :	Water Change — 10 - 15 % of water / 20 - 25 % of water
Salinity Level :	Other Condition :

TANK EQUIPMENT CHECK

COMPONENT	STATUS	CLEANING DATE	REPLACEMENT DATE	OBSERVATIONS
Filters :				
Pumps :				
Heaters :				
Lighting :				
Aquarium Walls				
Other Component				

NOTES : ....

....

....

....

Tank : ....   Date : ....

Fish Count : ....   Feeding : ....

FRESHWATER PARAMETERS

Water Temperature :	Nitrate Level :
pH Level :	Magnesium :
Ammonia :	Alkalinity : (Carbonate Hardness)
Nitrite Level :	Phosphates :
Calcium Level :	Water Change — 10 - 15 % of water — 20 - 25 % of water
Salinity Level :	Other Condition :

TANK EQUIPMENT CHECK

COMPONENT	STATUS	CLEANING DATE	REPLACEMENT DATE	OBSERVATIONS
Filters :				
Pumps :				
Heaters :				
Lighting :				
Aquarium Walls				
Other Component				

NOTES : ....

....

....

....

Tank : ....   Date : ....

Fish Count : ....   Feeding : ....

FRESHWATER PARAMETERS

Water Temperature :	Nitrate Level :
pH Level :	Magnesium :
Ammonia :	Alkalinity : (Carbonate Hardness)
Nitrite Level :	Phosphates :
Calcium Level :	Water Change — 10 - 15 % of water / 20 - 25 % of water
Salinity Level :	Other Condition :

TANK EQUIPMENT CHECK

COMPONENT	STATUS	CLEANING DATE	REPLACEMENT DATE	OBSERVATIONS
Filters :				
Pumps :				
Heaters :				
Lighting :				
Aquarium Walls				
Other Component				

NOTES : ....

....

....

....

Tank : .... Date : ....

Fish Count : .... Feeding : ....

FRESHWATER PARAMETERS

Water Temperature :	Nitrate Level :
pH Level :	Magnesium :
Ammonia :	Alkalinity : (Carbonate Hardness)
Nitrite Level :	Phosphates :
Calcium Level :	Water Change / 10 - 15 % of water / 20 - 25 % of water
Salinity Level :	Other Condition :

TANK EQUIPMENT CHECK

COMPONENT	STATUS	CLEANING DATE	REPLACEMENT DATE	OBSERVATIONS
Filters :				
Pumps :				
Heaters :				
Lighting :				
Aquarium Walls				
Other Component				

NOTES : ....

....

....

....

Tank : .... Date : ....

Fish Count : .... Feeding : ....

FRESHWATER PARAMETERS

Water Temperature :	Nitrate Level :
pH Level :	Magnesium :
Ammonia :	Alkalinity : (Carbonate Hardness)
Nitrite Level :	Phosphates :
Calcium Level :	Water Change — 10 - 15 % of water / 20 - 25 % of water
Salinity Level :	Other Condition :

TANK EQUIPMENT CHECK

COMPONENT	STATUS	CLEANING DATE	REPLACEMENT DATE	OBSERVATIONS
Filters :				
Pumps :				
Heaters :				
Lighting :				
Aquarium Walls				
Other Component				

NOTES : ....

....

....

....

Tank : .... Date : ....

Fish Count : .... Feeding : ....

FRESHWATER PARAMETERS

Water Temperature :	Nitrate Level :
pH Level :	Magnesium :
Ammonia :	Alkalinity : (Carbonate Hardness)
Nitrite Level :	Phosphates :
Calcium Level :	Water Change — 10 - 15 % of water / 20 - 25 % of water
Salinity Level :	Other Condition :

TANK EQUIPMENT CHECK

COMPONENT	STATUS	CLEANING DATE	REPLACEMENT DATE	OBSERVATIONS
Filters :				
Pumps :				
Heaters :				
Lighting :				
Aquarium Walls				
Other Component				

NOTES : ....

....

....

....

Tank : .... Date : ....

Fish Count : .... Feeding : ....

FRESHWATER PARAMETERS

Water Temperature :	Nitrate Level :
pH Level :	Magnesium :
Ammonia :	Alkalinity : (Carbonate Hardness)
Nitrite Level :	Phosphates :
Calcium Level :	Water Change — 10 - 15 % of water / 20 - 25 % of water
Salinity Level :	Other Condition :

TANK EQUIPMENT CHECK

COMPONENT	STATUS	CLEANING DATE	REPLACEMENT DATE	OBSERVATIONS
Filters :				
Pumps :				
Heaters :				
Lighting :				
Aquarium Walls				
Other Component				

NOTES : ....

....

....

....

Tank : ....   Date : ....

Fish Count : ....   Feeding : ....

FRESHWATER PARAMETERS

Water Temperature :	Nitrate Level :
pH Level :	Magnesium :
Ammonia :	Alkalinity : (Carbonate Hardness)
Nitrite Level :	Phosphates :
Calcium Level :	Water Change — 10 - 15 % of water / 20 - 25 % of water
Salinity Level :	Other Condition :

TANK EQUIPMENT CHECK

COMPONENT	STATUS	CLEANING DATE	REPLACEMENT DATE	OBSERVATIONS
Filters :				
Pumps :				
Heaters :				
Lighting :				
Aquarium Walls				
Other Component				

NOTES : ....

....

....

....

Tank : ....   Date : ....
Fish Count : ....   Feeding : ....

FRESHWATER PARAMETERS

Water Temperature :	Nitrate Level :
pH Level :	Magnesium :
Ammonia :	Alkalinity : (Carbonate Hardness)
Nitrite Level :	Phosphates :
Calcium Level :	Water Change 10 - 15 % of water 20 - 25 % of water
Salinity Level :	Other Condition :

TANK EQUIPMENT CHECK

COMPONENT	STATUS	CLEANING DATE	REPLACEMENT DATE	OBSERVATIONS
Filters :				
Pumps :				
Heaters :				
Lighting :				
Aquarium Walls				
Other Component				

NOTES : ....

....

....

....

Tank : .... Date : ....

Fish Count : .... Feeding : ....

FRESHWATER PARAMETERS

Water Temperature :	Nitrate Level :
pH Level :	Magnesium :
Ammonia :	Alkalinity : (Carbonate Hardness)
Nitrite Level :	Phosphates :
Calcium Level :	Water Change — 10 - 15 % of water / 20 - 25 % of water
Salinity Level :	Other Condition :

TANK EQUIPMENT CHECK

COMPONENT	STATUS	CLEANING DATE	REPLACEMENT DATE	OBSERVATIONS
Filters :				
Pumps :				
Heaters :				
Lighting :				
Aquarium Walls				
Other Component				

NOTES : ....

....

....

....

Tank : .... Date : ....

Fish Count : .... Feeding : ....

FRESHWATER PARAMETERS

Water Temperature :	Nitrate Level :
pH Level :	Magnesium :
Ammonia :	Alkalinity : (Carbonate Hardness)
Nitrite Level :	Phosphates :
Calcium Level :	Water Change — 10 - 15 % of water 20 - 25 % of water
Salinity Level :	Other Condition :

TANK EQUIPMENT CHECK

COMPONENT	STATUS	CLEANING DATE	REPLACEMENT DATE	OBSERVATIONS
Filters :				
Pumps :				
Heaters :				
Lighting :				
Aquarium Walls				
Other Component				

NOTES : ....

....

....

....

Tank : .... Date : ....

Fish Count : .... Feeding : ....

FRESHWATER PARAMETERS

Water Temperature :	Nitrate Level :
pH Level :	Magnesium :
Ammonia :	Alkalinity : (Carbonate Hardness)
Nitrite Level :	Phosphates :
Calcium Level :	Water Change / 10 - 15 % of water / 20 - 25 % of water
Salinity Level :	Other Condition :

TANK EQUIPMENT CHECK

COMPONENT	STATUS	CLEANING DATE	REPLACEMENT DATE	OBSERVATIONS
Filters :				
Pumps :				
Heaters :				
Lighting :				
Aquarium Walls				
Other Component				

NOTES : ....

....

....

....

Tank : .... Date : ....

Fish Count : .... Feeding : ....

FRESHWATER PARAMETERS

Water Temperature :	Nitrate Level :
pH Level :	Magnesium :
Ammonia :	Alkalinity : (Carbonate Hardness)
Nitrite Level :	Phosphates :
Calcium Level :	Water Change — 10 - 15 % of water 20 - 25 % of water
Salinity Level :	Other Condition :

TANK EQUIPMENT CHECK

COMPONENT	STATUS	CLEANING DATE	REPLACEMENT DATE	OBSERVATIONS
Filters :				
Pumps :				
Heaters :				
Lighting :				
Aquarium Walls				
Other Component				

NOTES : ....

....

....

....

Tank : .... Date : ....
Fish Count : .... Feeding : ....

FRESHWATER PARAMETERS

Water Temperature :	Nitrate Level :
pH Level :	Magnesium :
Ammonia :	Alkalinity : (Carbonate Hardness)
Nitrite Level :	Phosphates :
Calcium Level :	Water Change — 10 - 15 % of water / 20 - 25 % of water
Salinity Level :	Other Condition :

TANK EQUIPMENT CHECK

COMPONENT	STATUS	CLEANING DATE	REPLACEMENT DATE	OBSERVATIONS
Filters :				
Pumps :				
Heaters :				
Lighting :				
Aquarium Walls				
Other Component				

NOTES : ....

....

....

....

Tank : ....   Date : ....

Fish Count : ....   Feeding : ....

FRESHWATER PARAMETERS

Water Temperature :	Nitrate Level :
pH Level :	Magnesium :
Ammonia :	Alkalinity : (Carbonate Hardness)
Nitrite Level :	Phosphates :
Calcium Level :	Water Change 10 - 15 % of water / 20 - 25 % of water
Salinity Level :	Other Condition :

TANK EQUIPMENT CHECK

COMPONENT	STATUS	CLEANING DATE	REPLACEMENT DATE	OBSERVATIONS
Filters :				
Pumps :				
Heaters :				
Lighting :				
Aquarium Walls				
Other Component				

NOTES : ....

....

....

....

Tank : .... Date : ....

Fish Count : .... Feeding : ....

FRESHWATER PARAMETERS

Water Temperature :	Nitrate Level :
pH Level :	Magnesium :
Ammonia :	Alkalinity : (Carbonate Hardness)
Nitrite Level :	Phosphates :
Calcium Level :	Water Change — 10 - 15 % of water / 20 - 25 % of water
Salinity Level :	Other Condition :

TANK EQUIPMENT CHECK

COMPONENT	STATUS	CLEANING DATE	REPLACEMENT DATE	OBSERVATIONS
Filters :				
Pumps :				
Heaters :				
Lighting :				
Aquarium Walls				
Other Component				

NOTES : ....

....

....

....

Tank : .... Date : ....

Fish Count : .... Feeding : ....

FRESHWATER PARAMETERS

Water Temperature :	Nitrate Level :
pH Level :	Magnesium :
Ammonia :	Alkalinity : (Carbonate Hardness)
Nitrite Level :	Phosphates :
Calcium Level :	Water Change — 10 - 15 % of water / 20 - 25 % of water
Salinity Level :	Other Condition :

TANK EQUIPMENT CHECK

COMPONENT	STATUS	CLEANING DATE	REPLACEMENT DATE	OBSERVATIONS
Filters :				
Pumps :				
Heaters :				
Lighting :				
Aquarium Walls				
Other Component				

NOTES : ....

....

....

....

Tank : .... Date : ....

Fish Count : .... Feeding : ....

FRESHWATER PARAMETERS

Water Temperature :	Nitrate Level :
pH Level :	Magnesium :
Ammonia :	Alkalinity : (Carbonate Hardness)
Nitrite Level :	Phosphates :
Calcium Level :	Water Change — 10 - 15 % of water / 20 - 25 % of water
Salinity Level :	Other Condition :

TANK EQUIPMENT CHECK

COMPONENT	STATUS	CLEANING DATE	REPLACEMENT DATE	OBSERVATIONS
Filters :				
Pumps :				
Heaters :				
Lighting :				
Aquarium Walls				
Other Component				

NOTES : ....

....

....

....

Tank : .... Date : ....

Fish Count : .... Feeding : ....

FRESHWATER PARAMETERS

Water Temperature :	Nitrate Level :
pH Level :	Magnesium :
Ammonia :	Alkalinity : (Carbonate Hardness)
Nitrite Level :	Phosphates :
Calcium Level :	Water Change — 10 - 15 % of water 20 - 25 % of water
Salinity Level :	Other Condition :

TANK EQUIPMENT CHECK

COMPONENT	STATUS	CLEANING DATE	REPLACEMENT DATE	OBSERVATIONS
Filters :				
Pumps :				
Heaters :				
Lighting :				
Aquarium Walls				
Other Component				

NOTES : ....

....

....

Tank : .... Date : ....

Fish Count : .... Feeding : ....

FRESHWATER PARAMETERS

Water Temperature :	Nitrate Level :
pH Level :	Magnesium :
Ammonia :	Alkalinity : (Carbonate Hardness)
Nitrite Level :	Phosphates :
Calcium Level :	Water Change — 10 - 15 % of water / 20 - 25 % of water
Salinity Level :	Other Condition :

TANK EQUIPMENT CHECK

COMPONENT	STATUS	CLEANING DATE	REPLACEMENT DATE	OBSERVATIONS
Filters :				
Pumps :				
Heaters :				
Lighting :				
Aquarium Walls				
Other Component				

NOTES : ....

....

....

....

Tank : .... Date : ....

Fish Count : .... Feeding : ....

FRESHWATER PARAMETERS

Water Temperature :	Nitrate Level :
pH Level :	Magnesium :
Ammonia :	Alkalinity : (Carbonate Hardness)
Nitrite Level :	Phosphates :
Calcium Level :	Water Change — 10 - 15 % of water / 20 - 25 % of water
Salinity Level :	Other Condition :

TANK EQUIPMENT CHECK

COMPONENT	STATUS	CLEANING DATE	REPLACEMENT DATE	OBSERVATIONS
Filters :				
Pumps :				
Heaters :				
Lighting :				
Aquarium Walls				
Other Component				

NOTES : ....

....

....

....

Tank : .... Date : ....

Fish Count : .... Feeding : ....

FRESHWATER PARAMETERS

Water Temperature :	Nitrate Level :
pH Level :	Magnesium :
Ammonia :	Alkalinity : (Carbonate Hardness)
Nitrite Level :	Phosphates :
Calcium Level :	Water Change — 10 - 15 % of water / 20 - 25 % of water
Salinity Level :	Other Condition :

TANK EQUIPMENT CHECK

COMPONENT	STATUS	CLEANING DATE	REPLACEMENT DATE	OBSERVATIONS
Filters :				
Pumps :				
Heaters :				
Lighting :				
Aquarium Walls				
Other Component				

NOTES : ....

....

....

....

Tank : .... Date : ....

Fish Count : .... Feeding : ....

FRESHWATER PARAMETERS

Water Temperature :	Nitrate Level :
pH Level :	Magnesium :
Ammonia :	Alkalinity : (Carbonate Hardness)
Nitrite Level :	Phosphates :
Calcium Level :	Water Change — 10 - 15 % of water 20 - 25 % of water
Salinity Level :	Other Condition :

TANK EQUIPMENT CHECK

COMPONENT	STATUS	CLEANING DATE	REPLACEMENT DATE	OBSERVATIONS
Filters :				
Pumps :				
Heaters :				
Lighting :				
Aquarium Walls				
Other Component				

NOTES : ....

....

....

....

Tank : .... Date : ....

Fish Count : .... Feeding : ....

FRESHWATER PARAMETERS

Water Temperature :	Nitrate Level :
pH Level :	Magnesium :
Ammonia :	Alkalinity : (Carbonate Hardness)
Nitrite Level :	Phosphates :
Calcium Level :	Water Change — 10 - 15 % of water / 20 - 25 % of water
Salinity Level :	Other Condition :

TANK EQUIPMENT CHECK

COMPONENT	STATUS	CLEANING DATE	REPLACEMENT DATE	OBSERVATIONS
Filters :				
Pumps :				
Heaters :				
Lighting :				
Aquarium Walls				
Other Component				

NOTES : ....

....

....

....

Tank : .... Date : ....

Fish Count : .... Feeding : ....

FRESHWATER PARAMETERS

Water Temperature :	Nitrate Level :
pH Level :	Magnesium :
Ammonia :	Alkalinity : (Carbonate Hardness)
Nitrite Level :	Phosphates :
Calcium Level :	Water Change — 10 - 15 % of water / 20 - 25 % of water
Salinity Level :	Other Condition :

TANK EQUIPMENT CHECK

COMPONENT	STATUS	CLEANING DATE	REPLACEMENT DATE	OBSERVATIONS
Filters :				
Pumps :				
Heaters :				
Lighting :				
Aquarium Walls				
Other Component				

NOTES : ....

....

....

....

Tank : ....   Date : ....

Fish Count : ....   Feeding : ....

FRESHWATER PARAMETERS

Water Temperature :	Nitrate Level :
pH Level :	Magnesium :
Ammonia :	Alkalinity : (Carbonate Hardness)
Nitrite Level :	Phosphates :
Calcium Level :	Water Change — 10 - 15 % of water / 20 - 25 % of water
Salinity Level :	Other Condition :

TANK EQUIPMENT CHECK

COMPONENT	STATUS	CLEANING DATE	REPLACEMENT DATE	OBSERVATIONS
Filters :				
Pumps :				
Heaters :				
Lighting :				
Aquarium Walls				
Other Component				

NOTES : ....

....

....

....

Tank : .... Date : ....

Fish Count : .... Feeding : ....

FRESHWATER PARAMETERS

Water Temperature :	Nitrate Level :
pH Level :	Magnesium :
Ammonia :	Alkalinity : (Carbonate Hardness)
Nitrite Level :	Phosphates :
Calcium Level :	Water Change / 10 - 15 % of water / 20 - 25 % of water
Salinity Level :	Other Condition :

TANK EQUIPMENT CHECK

COMPONENT	STATUS	CLEANING DATE	REPLACEMENT DATE	OBSERVATIONS
Filters :				
Pumps :				
Heaters :				
Lighting :				
Aquarium Walls				
Other Component				

NOTES : ....

....

....

....

Tank : .... Date : ....

Fish Count : .... Feeding : ....

FRESHWATER PARAMETERS

Water Temperature :	Nitrate Level :
pH Level :	Magnesium :
Ammonia :	Alkalinity : (Carbonate Hardness)
Nitrite Level :	Phosphates :
Calcium Level :	Water Change — 10 - 15 % of water / 20 - 25 % of water
Salinity Level :	Other Condition :

TANK EQUIPMENT CHECK

COMPONENT	STATUS	CLEANING DATE	REPLACEMENT DATE	OBSERVATIONS
Filters :				
Pumps :				
Heaters :				
Lighting :				
Aquarium Walls				
Other Component				

NOTES : ....
....
....
....

Tank : .... Date : ....

Fish Count : .... Feeding : ....

FRESHWATER PARAMETERS

Water Temperature :	Nitrate Level :
pH Level :	Magnesium :
Ammonia :	Alkalinity : (Carbonate Hardness)
Nitrite Level :	Phosphates :
Calcium Level :	Water Change / 10 - 15 % of water / 20 - 25 % of water
Salinity Level :	Other Condition :

TANK EQUIPMENT CHECK

COMPONENT	STATUS	CLEANING DATE	REPLACEMENT DATE	OBSERVATIONS
Filters :				
Pumps :				
Heaters :				
Lighting :				
Aquarium Walls				
Other Component				

NOTES : ....

....

....

....

Tank : .... Date : ....
Fish Count : .... Feeding : ....

FRESHWATER PARAMETERS

Water Temperature :	Nitrate Level :
pH Level :	Magnesium :
Ammonia :	Alkalinity : (Carbonate Hardness)
Nitrite Level :	Phosphates :
Calcium Level :	Water Change — 10 - 15 % of water / 20 - 25 % of water
Salinity Level :	Other Condition :

TANK EQUIPMENT CHECK

COMPONENT	STATUS	CLEANING DATE	REPLACEMENT DATE	OBSERVATIONS
Filters :				
Pumps :				
Heaters :				
Lighting :				
Aquarium Walls				
Other Component				

NOTES : ....
....
....
....

Tank : .... Date : ....

Fish Count : .... Feeding : ....

FRESHWATER PARAMETERS

Water Temperature :	Nitrate Level :
pH Level :	Magnesium :
Ammonia :	Alkalinity : (Carbonate Hardness)
Nitrite Level :	Phosphates :
Calcium Level :	Water Change — 10 - 15 % of water / 20 - 25 % of water
Salinity Level :	Other Condition :

TANK EQUIPMENT CHECK

COMPONENT	STATUS	CLEANING DATE	REPLACEMENT DATE	OBSERVATIONS
Filters :				
Pumps :				
Heaters :				
Lighting :				
Aquarium Walls				
Other Component				

NOTES : ....

....

....

....

Tank : ....   Date : ....

Fish Count : ....   Feeding : ....

FRESHWATER PARAMETERS

Water Temperature :	Nitrate Level :
pH Level :	Magnesium :
Ammonia :	Alkalinity : (Carbonate Hardness)
Nitrite Level :	Phosphates :
Calcium Level :	Water Change 10 - 15 % of water 20 - 25 % of water
Salinity Level :	Other Condition :

TANK EQUIPMENT CHECK

COMPONENT	STATUS	CLEANING DATE	REPLACEMENT DATE	OBSERVATIONS
Filters :				
Pumps :				
Heaters :				
Lighting :				
Aquarium Walls				
Other Component				

NOTES : ....

....

....

....

Tank : .... Date : ....

Fish Count : .... Feeding : ....

FRESHWATER PARAMETERS

Water Temperature :	Nitrate Level :
pH Level :	Magnesium :
Ammonia :	Alkalinity : (Carbonate Hardness)
Nitrite Level :	Phosphates :
Calcium Level :	Water Change — 10 - 15 % of water / 20 - 25 % of water
Salinity Level :	Other Condition :

TANK EQUIPMENT CHECK

COMPONENT	STATUS	CLEANING DATE	REPLACEMENT DATE	OBSERVATIONS
Filters :				
Pumps :				
Heaters :				
Lighting :				
Aquarium Walls				
Other Component				

NOTES : ....

....

....

....

Tank : .... Date : ....

Fish Count : .... Feeding : ....

FRESHWATER PARAMETERS

Water Temperature :	Nitrate Level :
pH Level :	Magnesium :
Ammonia :	Alkalinity : (Carbonate Hardness)
Nitrite Level :	Phosphates :
Calcium Level :	Water Change — 10 - 15 % of water / 20 - 25 % of water
Salinity Level :	Other Condition :

TANK EQUIPMENT CHECK

COMPONENT	STATUS	CLEANING DATE	REPLACEMENT DATE	OBSERVATIONS
Filters :				
Pumps :				
Heaters :				
Lighting :				
Aquarium Walls				
Other Component				

NOTES : ....

....

....

....

Tank : .... Date : ....

Fish Count : .... Feeding : ....

FRESHWATER PARAMETERS

Water Temperature :	Nitrate Level :
pH Level :	Magnesium :
Ammonia :	Alkalinity : (Carbonate Hardness)
Nitrite Level :	Phosphates :
Calcium Level :	Water Change — 10 - 15 % of water / 20 - 25 % of water
Salinity Level :	Other Condition :

TANK EQUIPMENT CHECK

COMPONENT	STATUS	CLEANING DATE	REPLACEMENT DATE	OBSERVATIONS
Filters :				
Pumps :				
Heaters :				
Lighting :				
Aquarium Walls				
Other Component				

NOTES : ....

....

....

....

Tank : .... Date : ....
Fish Count : .... Feeding : ....

FRESHWATER PARAMETERS

Water Temperature :	Nitrate Level :
pH Level :	Magnesium :
Ammonia :	Alkalinity : (Carbonate Hardness)
Nitrite Level :	Phosphates :
Calcium Level :	Water Change — 10 - 15 % of water / 20 - 25 % of water
Salinity Level :	Other Condition :

TANK EQUIPMENT CHECK

COMPONENT	STATUS	CLEANING DATE	REPLACEMENT DATE	OBSERVATIONS
Filters :				
Pumps :				
Heaters :				
Lighting :				
Aquarium Walls				
Other Component				

NOTES : ....
....
....
....

Tank : .... Date : ....
Fish Count : .... Feeding : ....

FRESHWATER PARAMETERS

Water Temperature :	Nitrate Level :
pH Level :	Magnesium :
Ammonia :	Alkalinity : (Carbonate Hardness)
Nitrite Level :	Phosphates :
Calcium Level :	Water Change / 10 - 15 % of water / 20 - 25 % of water
Salinity Level :	Other Condition :

TANK EQUIPMENT CHECK

COMPONENT	STATUS	CLEANING DATE	REPLACEMENT DATE	OBSERVATIONS
Filters :				
Pumps :				
Heaters :				
Lighting :				
Aquarium Walls				
Other Component				

NOTES : ....
....
....
....

Tank : .... Date : ....

Fish Count : .... Feeding : ....

FRESHWATER PARAMETERS

Water Temperature :	Nitrate Level :
pH Level :	Magnesium :
Ammonia :	Alkalinity : (Carbonate Hardness)
Nitrite Level :	Phosphates :
Calcium Level :	Water Change — 10 - 15 % of water / 20 - 25 % of water
Salinity Level :	Other Condition :

TANK EQUIPMENT CHECK

COMPONENT	STATUS	CLEANING DATE	REPLACEMENT DATE	OBSERVATIONS
Filters :				
Pumps :				
Heaters :				
Lighting :				
Aquarium Walls				
Other Component				

NOTES : ....

....

....

....

Tank : .... Date : ....

Fish Count : .... Feeding : ....

FRESHWATER PARAMETERS

Water Temperature :	Nitrate Level :
pH Level :	Magnesium :
Ammonia :	Alkalinity : (Carbonate Hardness)
Nitrite Level :	Phosphates :
Calcium Level :	Water Change — 10 - 15 % of water / 20 - 25 % of water
Salinity Level :	Other Condition :

TANK EQUIPMENT CHECK

COMPONENT	STATUS	CLEANING DATE	REPLACEMENT DATE	OBSERVATIONS
Filters :				
Pumps :				
Heaters :				
Lighting :				
Aquarium Walls				
Other Component				

NOTES : ....

....

....

....

Tank : ....   Date : ....

Fish Count : ....   Feeding : ....

FRESHWATER PARAMETERS

Water Temperature :	Nitrate Level :
pH Level :	Magnesium :
Ammonia :	Alkalinity : (Carbonate Hardness)
Nitrite Level :	Phosphates :
Calcium Level :	Water Change 10 - 15 % of water 20 - 25 % of water
Salinity Level :	Other Condition :

TANK EQUIPMENT CHECK

COMPONENT	STATUS	CLEANING DATE	REPLACEMENT DATE	OBSERVATIONS
Filters :				
Pumps :				
Heaters :				
Lighting :				
Aquarium Walls				
Other Component				

NOTES : ....

....

....

....

Tank : .... Date : ....
Fish Count : .... Feeding : ....

FRESHWATER PARAMETERS

Water Temperature :	Nitrate Level :
pH Level :	Magnesium :
Ammonia :	Alkalinity : (Carbonate Hardness)
Nitrite Level :	Phosphates :
Calcium Level :	Water Change / 10 - 15 % of water / 20 - 25 % of water
Salinity Level :	Other Condition :

TANK EQUIPMENT CHECK

COMPONENT	STATUS	CLEANING DATE	REPLACEMENT DATE	OBSERVATIONS
Filters :				
Pumps :				
Heaters :				
Lighting :				
Aquarium Walls				
Other Component				

NOTES : ....
....
....
....

Tank : .... Date : ....

Fish Count : .... Feeding : ....

FRESHWATER PARAMETERS

Water Temperature :	Nitrate Level :
pH Level :	Magnesium :
Ammonia :	Alkalinity : (Carbonate Hardness)
Nitrite Level :	Phosphates :
Calcium Level :	Water Change — 10 - 15 % of water / 20 - 25 % of water
Salinity Level :	Other Condition :

TANK EQUIPMENT CHECK

COMPONENT	STATUS	CLEANING DATE	REPLACEMENT DATE	OBSERVATIONS
Filters :				
Pumps :				
Heaters :				
Lighting :				
Aquarium Walls				
Other Component				

NOTES : ....

....

....

....

Tank : ....   Date : ....

Fish Count : ....   Feeding : ....

FRESHWATER PARAMETERS

Water Temperature :	Nitrate Level :
pH Level :	Magnesium :
Ammonia :	Alkalinity : (Carbonate Hardness)
Nitrite Level :	Phosphates :
Calcium Level :	Water Change — 10 - 15 % of water / 20 - 25 % of water
Salinity Level :	Other Condition :

TANK EQUIPMENT CHECK

COMPONENT	STATUS	CLEANING DATE	REPLACEMENT DATE	OBSERVATIONS
Filters :				
Pumps :				
Heaters :				
Lighting :				
Aquarium Walls				
Other Component				

NOTES : ....

....

....

....

Tank : ....   Date : ....

Fish Count : ....   Feeding : ....

FRESHWATER PARAMETERS

Water Temperature :	Nitrate Level :
pH Level :	Magnesium :
Ammonia :	Alkalinity : (Carbonate Hardness)
Nitrite Level :	Phosphates :
Calcium Level :	Water Change — 10 - 15 % of water / 20 - 25 % of water
Salinity Level :	Other Condition :

TANK EQUIPMENT CHECK

COMPONENT	STATUS	CLEANING DATE	REPLACEMENT DATE	OBSERVATIONS
Filters :				
Pumps :				
Heaters :				
Lighting :				
Aquarium Walls				
Other Component				

NOTES : ....

....

....

....

Tank : .... Date : ....

Fish Count : .... Feeding : ....

FRESHWATER PARAMETERS

Water Temperature :	Nitrate Level :
pH Level :	Magnesium :
Ammonia :	Alkalinity : (Carbonate Hardness)
Nitrite Level :	Phosphates :
Calcium Level :	Water Change / 10 - 15 % of water / 20 - 25 % of water
Salinity Level :	Other Condition :

TANK EQUIPMENT CHECK

COMPONENT	STATUS	CLEANING DATE	REPLACEMENT DATE	OBSERVATIONS
Filters :				
Pumps :				
Heaters :				
Lighting :				
Aquarium Walls				
Other Component				

NOTES : ....

....

....

....

Tank : .... Date : ....

Fish Count : .... Feeding : ....

FRESHWATER PARAMETERS

Water Temperature :	Nitrate Level :
pH Level :	Magnesium :
Ammonia :	Alkalinity : (Carbonate Hardness)
Nitrite Level :	Phosphates :
Calcium Level :	Water Change — 10 - 15 % of water / 20 - 25 % of water
Salinity Level :	Other Condition :

TANK EQUIPMENT CHECK

COMPONENT	STATUS	CLEANING DATE	REPLACEMENT DATE	OBSERVATIONS
Filters :				
Pumps :				
Heaters :				
Lighting :				
Aquarium Walls				
Other Component				

NOTES : ....

....

....

Tank : .... Date : ....
Fish Count : .... Feeding : ....

FRESHWATER PARAMETERS

Water Temperature :	Nitrate Level :
pH Level :	Magnesium :
Ammonia :	Alkalinity : (Carbonate Hardness)
Nitrite Level :	Phosphates :
Calcium Level :	Water Change / 10 - 15 % of water
	Water Change / 20 - 25 % of water
Salinity Level :	Other Condition :

TANK EQUIPMENT CHECK

COMPONENT	STATUS	CLEANING DATE	REPLACEMENT DATE	OBSERVATIONS
Filters :				
Pumps :				
Heaters :				
Lighting :				
Aquarium Walls				
Other Component				

NOTES : ....

....

....

....

Tank : .... Date : ....

Fish Count : .... Feeding : ....

FRESHWATER PARAMETERS

Water Temperature :	Nitrate Level :
pH Level :	Magnesium :
Ammonia :	Alkalinity : (Carbonate Hardness)
Nitrite Level :	Phosphates :
Calcium Level :	Water Change — 10 - 15 % of water : __ / 20 - 25 % of water : __
Salinity Level :	Other Condition :

TANK EQUIPMENT CHECK

COMPONENT	STATUS	CLEANING DATE	REPLACEMENT DATE	OBSERVATIONS
Filters :				
Pumps :				
Heaters :				
Lighting :				
Aquarium Walls				
Other Component				

NOTES : ....

....

....

....

Tank : .... Date : ....

Fish Count : .... Feeding : ....

FRESHWATER PARAMETERS	
Water Temperature :	Nitrate Level :
pH Level :	Magnesium :
Ammonia :	Alkalinity : (Carbonate Hardness)
Nitrite Level :	Phosphates :
Calcium Level :	Water Change — 10 - 15 % of water / 20 - 25 % of water
Salinity Level :	Other Condition :

TANK EQUIPMENT CHECK

COMPONENT	STATUS	CLEANING DATE	REPLACEMENT DATE	OBSERVATIONS
Filters :				
Pumps :				
Heaters :				
Lighting :				
Aquarium Walls				
Other Component				

NOTES : ....

....

....

....

Tank : .... Date : ....
Fish Count : .... Feeding : ....

FRESHWATER PARAMETERS

Water Temperature :	Nitrate Level :
pH Level :	Magnesium :
Ammonia :	Alkalinity : (Carbonate Hardness)
Nitrite Level :	Phosphates :
Calcium Level :	Water Change — 10 - 15 % of water / 20 - 25 % of water
Salinity Level :	Other Condition :

TANK EQUIPMENT CHECK

COMPONENT	STATUS	CLEANING DATE	REPLACEMENT DATE	OBSERVATIONS
Filters :				
Pumps :				
Heaters :				
Lighting :				
Aquarium Walls				
Other Component				

NOTES : ....
....
....

Tank : ....   Date : ....

Fish Count : ....   Feeding : ....

FRESHWATER PARAMETERS

Water Temperature :	Nitrate Level :
pH Level :	Magnesium :
Ammonia :	Alkalinity : (Carbonate Hardness)
Nitrite Level :	Phosphates :
Calcium Level :	Water Change — 10 - 15 % of water / 20 - 25 % of water
Salinity Level :	Other Condition :

TANK EQUIPMENT CHECK

COMPONENT	STATUS	CLEANING DATE	REPLACEMENT DATE	OBSERVATIONS
Filters :				
Pumps :				
Heaters :				
Lighting :				
Aquarium Walls				
Other Component				

NOTES : ....

....

....

....

Tank : .... Date : ....
Fish Count : .... Feeding : ....

FRESHWATER PARAMETERS

Water Temperature :	Nitrate Level :
pH Level :	Magnesium :
Ammonia :	Alkalinity : (Carbonate Hardness)
Nitrite Level :	Phosphates :
Calcium Level :	Water Change — 10 - 15 % of water / 20 - 25 % of water
Salinity Level :	Other Condition :

TANK EQUIPMENT CHECK

COMPONENT	STATUS	CLEANING DATE	REPLACEMENT DATE	OBSERVATIONS
Filters :				
Pumps :				
Heaters :				
Lighting :				
Aquarium Walls				
Other Component				

NOTES : ....

....

....

....

Tank : .... Date : ....

Fish Count : .... Feeding : ....

FRESHWATER PARAMETERS

Water Temperature :	Nitrate Level :
pH Level :	Magnesium :
Ammonia :	Alkalinity : (Carbonate Hardness)
Nitrite Level :	Phosphates :
Calcium Level :	Water Change	10 - 15 % of water	
		20 - 25 % of water	
Salinity Level :	Other Condition :

TANK EQUIPMENT CHECK

COMPONENT	STATUS	CLEANING DATE	REPLACEMENT DATE	OBSERVATIONS
Filters :				
Pumps :				
Heaters :				
Lighting :				
Aquarium Walls				
Other Component				

NOTES : ....

....

....

....

Tank : .... Date : ....

Fish Count : .... Feeding : ....

FRESHWATER PARAMETERS

Water Temperature :	Nitrate Level :
pH Level :	Magnesium :
Ammonia :	Alkalinity : (Carbonate Hardness)
Nitrite Level :	Phosphates :
Calcium Level :	Water Change — 10 - 15 % of water / 20 - 25 % of water
Salinity Level :	Other Condition :

TANK EQUIPMENT CHECK

COMPONENT	STATUS	CLEANING DATE	REPLACEMENT DATE	OBSERVATIONS
Filters :				
Pumps :				
Heaters :				
Lighting :				
Aquarium Walls				
Other Component				

NOTES : ....

....

....

Tank : ....   Date : ....

Fish Count : ....   Feeding : ....

FRESHWATER PARAMETERS

Water Temperature :	Nitrate Level :
pH Level :	Magnesium :
Ammonia :	Alkalinity : (Carbonate Hardness)
Nitrite Level :	Phosphates :
Calcium Level :	Water Change — 10 - 15 % of water / 20 - 25 % of water
Salinity Level :	Other Condition :

TANK EQUIPMENT CHECK

COMPONENT	STATUS	CLEANING DATE	REPLACEMENT DATE	OBSERVATIONS
Filters :				
Pumps :				
Heaters :				
Lighting :				
Aquarium Walls				
Other Component				

NOTES : ....

....

....

....

Tank : .... Date : ....

Fish Count : .... Feeding : ....

FRESHWATER PARAMETERS	
Water Temperature :	Nitrate Level :
pH Level :	Magnesium :
Ammonia :	Alkalinity : (Carbonate Hardness)
Nitrite Level :	Phosphates :
Calcium Level :	Water Change — 10 - 15 % of water / 20 - 25 % of water
Salinity Level :	Other Condition :

TANK EQUIPMENT CHECK

COMPONENT	STATUS	CLEANING DATE	REPLACEMENT DATE	OBSERVATIONS
Filters :				
Pumps :				
Heaters :				
Lighting :				
Aquarium Walls				
Other Component				

NOTES : ....

....

....

....

Tank : .... Date : ....

Fish Count : .... Feeding : ....

FRESHWATER PARAMETERS

Water Temperature :	Nitrate Level :
pH Level :	Magnesium :
Ammonia :	Alkalinity : (Carbonate Hardness)
Nitrite Level :	Phosphates :
Calcium Level :	Water Change — 10 - 15 % of water / 20 - 25 % of water
Salinity Level :	Other Condition :

TANK EQUIPMENT CHECK

COMPONENT	STATUS	CLEANING DATE	REPLACEMENT DATE	OBSERVATIONS
Filters :				
Pumps :				
Heaters :				
Lighting :				
Aquarium Walls				
Other Component				

NOTES : ....

....

....

....

Tank : ....   Date : ....

Fish Count : ....   Feeding : ....

FRESHWATER PARAMETERS

Water Temperature :	Nitrate Level :
pH Level :	Magnesium :
Ammonia :	Alkalinity : (Carbonate Hardness)
Nitrite Level :	Phosphates :
Calcium Level :	Water Change — 10 - 15 % of water / 20 - 25 % of water
Salinity Level :	Other Condition :

TANK EQUIPMENT CHECK

COMPONENT	STATUS	CLEANING DATE	REPLACEMENT DATE	OBSERVATIONS
Filters :				
Pumps :				
Heaters :				
Lighting :				
Aquarium Walls				
Other Component				

NOTES : ....

....

....

....

Tank : .... Date : ....

Fish Count : .... Feeding : ....

FRESHWATER PARAMETERS

Water Temperature :	Nitrate Level :
pH Level :	Magnesium :
Ammonia :	Alkalinity : (Carbonate Hardness)
Nitrite Level :	Phosphates :
Calcium Level :	Water Change / 10 - 15 % of water / 20 - 25 % of water
Salinity Level :	Other Condition :

TANK EQUIPMENT CHECK

COMPONENT	STATUS	CLEANING DATE	REPLACEMENT DATE	OBSERVATIONS
Filters :				
Pumps :				
Heaters :				
Lighting :				
Aquarium Walls				
Other Component				

NOTES : ....

....

....

....

Tank : .... Date : ....

Fish Count : .... Feeding : ....

FRESHWATER PARAMETERS

Water Temperature :	Nitrate Level :
pH Level :	Magnesium :
Ammonia :	Alkalinity : (Carbonate Hardness)
Nitrite Level :	Phosphates :
Calcium Level :	Water Change — 10 - 15 % of water / 20 - 25 % of water
Salinity Level :	Other Condition :

TANK EQUIPMENT CHECK

COMPONENT	STATUS	CLEANING DATE	REPLACEMENT DATE	OBSERVATIONS
Filters :				
Pumps :				
Heaters :				
Lighting :				
Aquarium Walls				
Other Component				

NOTES : ....
....
....
....

Tank : .... Date : ....

Fish Count : .... Feeding : ....

FRESHWATER PARAMETERS

Water Temperature :	Nitrate Level :
pH Level :	Magnesium :
Ammonia :	Alkalinity : (Carbonate Hardness)
Nitrite Level :	Phosphates :
Calcium Level :	Water Change — 10 - 15 % of water / 20 - 25 % of water
Salinity Level :	Other Condition :

TANK EQUIPMENT CHECK

COMPONENT	STATUS	CLEANING DATE	REPLACEMENT DATE	OBSERVATIONS
Filters :				
Pumps :				
Heaters :				
Lighting :				
Aquarium Walls				
Other Component				

NOTES : ....

....

....

....

Tank : .... Date : ....

Fish Count : .... Feeding : ....

FRESHWATER PARAMETERS

Water Temperature :	Nitrate Level :
pH Level :	Magnesium :
Ammonia :	Alkalinity : (Carbonate Hardness)
Nitrite Level :	Phosphates :
Calcium Level :	Water Change — 10 - 15 % of water / 20 - 25 % of water
Salinity Level :	Other Condition :

TANK EQUIPMENT CHECK

COMPONENT	STATUS	CLEANING DATE	REPLACEMENT DATE	OBSERVATIONS
Filters :				
Pumps :				
Heaters :				
Lighting :				
Aquarium Walls				
Other Component				

NOTES : ....

....

....

....

Tank : ....   Date : ....

Fish Count : ....   Feeding : ....

FRESHWATER PARAMETERS

Water Temperature :	Nitrate Level :
pH Level :	Magnesium :
Ammonia :	Alkalinity : (Carbonate Hardness)
Nitrite Level :	Phosphates :
Calcium Level :	Water Change / 10 - 15 % of water / 20 - 25 % of water
Salinity Level :	Other Condition :

TANK EQUIPMENT CHECK

COMPONENT	STATUS	CLEANING DATE	REPLACEMENT DATE	OBSERVATIONS
Filters :				
Pumps :				
Heaters :				
Lighting :				
Aquarium Walls				
Other Component				

NOTES : ....

....

....

....

Tank : .... Date : ....

Fish Count : .... Feeding : ....

FRESHWATER PARAMETERS

Water Temperature :	Nitrate Level :
pH Level :	Magnesium :
Ammonia :	Alkalinity : (Carbonate Hardness)
Nitrite Level :	Phosphates :
Calcium Level :	Water Change — 10 - 15 % of water / 20 - 25 % of water
Salinity Level :	Other Condition :

TANK EQUIPMENT CHECK

COMPONENT	STATUS	CLEANING DATE	REPLACEMENT DATE	OBSERVATIONS
Filters :				
Pumps :				
Heaters :				
Lighting :				
Aquarium Walls				
Other Component				

NOTES : ....

....

....

....

Tank : .... Date : ....

Fish Count : .... Feeding : ....

FRESHWATER PARAMETERS

Water Temperature :	Nitrate Level :
pH Level :	Magnesium :
Ammonia :	Alkalinity : (Carbonate Hardness)
Nitrite Level :	Phosphates :
Calcium Level :	Water Change — 10 - 15 % of water / 20 - 25 % of water
Salinity Level :	Other Condition :

TANK EQUIPMENT CHECK

COMPONENT	STATUS	CLEANING DATE	REPLACEMENT DATE	OBSERVATIONS
Filters :				
Pumps :				
Heaters :				
Lighting :				
Aquarium Walls				
Other Component				

NOTES : ....

....

....

....

Tank : .... Date : ....

Fish Count : .... Feeding : ....

FRESHWATER PARAMETERS

Water Temperature :	Nitrate Level :
pH Level :	Magnesium :
Ammonia :	Alkalinity : (Carbonate Hardness)
Nitrite Level :	Phosphates :
Calcium Level :	Water Change / 10 - 15 % of water / 20 - 25 % of water
Salinity Level :	Other Condition :

TANK EQUIPMENT CHECK

COMPONENT	STATUS	CLEANING DATE	REPLACEMENT DATE	OBSERVATIONS
Filters :				
Pumps :				
Heaters :				
Lighting :				
Aquarium Walls				
Other Component				

NOTES : ....

....

....

....

Tank : .... Date : ....

Fish Count : .... Feeding : ....

FRESHWATER PARAMETERS

Water Temperature :	Nitrate Level :
pH Level :	Magnesium :
Ammonia :	Alkalinity : (Carbonate Hardness)
Nitrite Level :	Phosphates :
Calcium Level :	Water Change — 10 - 15 % of water / 20 - 25 % of water
Salinity Level :	Other Condition :

TANK EQUIPMENT CHECK

COMPONENT	STATUS	CLEANING DATE	REPLACEMENT DATE	OBSERVATIONS
Filters :				
Pumps :				
Heaters :				
Lighting :				
Aquarium Walls				
Other Component				

NOTES : ....

....

....

....

Tank : .... Date : ....

Fish Count : .... Feeding : ....

FRESHWATER PARAMETERS

Water Temperature :	Nitrate Level :
pH Level :	Magnesium :
Ammonia :	Alkalinity : (Carbonate Hardness)
Nitrite Level :	Phosphates :
Calcium Level :	Water Change — 10 - 15 % of water / 20 - 25 % of water
Salinity Level :	Other Condition :

TANK EQUIPMENT CHECK

COMPONENT	STATUS	CLEANING DATE	REPLACEMENT DATE	OBSERVATIONS
Filters :				
Pumps :				
Heaters :				
Lighting :				
Aquarium Walls				
Other Component				

NOTES : ....

....

....

....

Tank : .... Date : ....

Fish Count : .... Feeding : ....

FRESHWATER PARAMETERS

Water Temperature :	Nitrate Level :
pH Level :	Magnesium :
Ammonia :	Alkalinity : (Carbonate Hardness)
Nitrite Level :	Phosphates :
Calcium Level :	Water Change / 10 - 15 % of water / 20 - 25 % of water
Salinity Level :	Other Condition :

TANK EQUIPMENT CHECK

COMPONENT	STATUS	CLEANING DATE	REPLACEMENT DATE	OBSERVATIONS
Filters :				
Pumps :				
Heaters :				
Lighting :				
Aquarium Walls				
Other Component				

NOTES : ....

....

....

....

Tank : .... Date : ....

Fish Count : .... Feeding : ....

FRESHWATER PARAMETERS

Water Temperature :	Nitrate Level :
pH Level :	Magnesium :
Ammonia :	Alkalinity : (Carbonate Hardness)
Nitrite Level :	Phosphates :
Calcium Level :	Water Change — 10 - 15 % of water / 20 - 25 % of water
Salinity Level :	Other Condition :

TANK EQUIPMENT CHECK

COMPONENT	STATUS	CLEANING DATE	REPLACEMENT DATE	OBSERVATIONS
Filters :				
Pumps :				
Heaters :				
Lighting :				
Aquarium Walls				
Other Component				

NOTES : ....

....

....

....

Tank : ....   Date : ....
Fish Count : ....   Feeding : ....

FRESHWATER PARAMETERS

Water Temperature :	Nitrate Level :
pH Level :	Magnesium :
Ammonia :	Alkalinity : (Carbonate Hardness)
Nitrite Level :	Phosphates :
Calcium Level :	Water Change — 10 - 15 % of water / 20 - 25 % of water
Salinity Level :	Other Condition :

TANK EQUIPMENT CHECK

COMPONENT	STATUS	CLEANING DATE	REPLACEMENT DATE	OBSERVATIONS
Filters :				
Pumps :				
Heaters :				
Lighting :				
Aquarium Walls				
Other Component				

NOTES : ....

....

....

....

Tank : ....   Date : ....

Fish Count : ....   Feeding : ....

FRESHWATER PARAMETERS

Water Temperature :	Nitrate Level :
pH Level :	Magnesium :
Ammonia :	Alkalinity : (Carbonate Hardness)
Nitrite Level :	Phosphates :
Calcium Level :	Water Change — 10 - 15 % of water / 20 - 25 % of water
Salinity Level :	Other Condition :

TANK EQUIPMENT CHECK

COMPONENT	STATUS	CLEANING DATE	REPLACEMENT DATE	OBSERVATIONS
Filters :				
Pumps :				
Heaters :				
Lighting :				
Aquarium Walls				
Other Component				

NOTES : ....

....

....

....

Tank : .... Date : ....
Fish Count : .... Feeding : ....

FRESHWATER PARAMETERS

Water Temperature :	Nitrate Level :
pH Level :	Magnesium :
Ammonia :	Alkalinity : (Carbonate Hardness)
Nitrite Level :	Phosphates :
Calcium Level :	Water Change — 10 - 15 % of water / 20 - 25 % of water
Salinity Level :	Other Condition :

TANK EQUIPMENT CHECK

COMPONENT	STATUS	CLEANING DATE	REPLACEMENT DATE	OBSERVATIONS
Filters :				
Pumps :				
Heaters :				
Lighting :				
Aquarium Walls				
Other Component				

NOTES : ....

....

....

....

Tank : .... Date : ....

Fish Count : .... Feeding : ....

FRESHWATER PARAMETERS

Water Temperature :	Nitrate Level :
pH Level :	Magnesium :
Ammonia :	Alkalinity : (Carbonate Hardness)
Nitrite Level :	Phosphates :
Calcium Level :	Water Change / 10 - 15 % of water / 20 - 25 % of water
Salinity Level :	Other Condition :

TANK EQUIPMENT CHECK

COMPONENT	STATUS	CLEANING DATE	REPLACEMENT DATE	OBSERVATIONS
Filters :				
Pumps :				
Heaters :				
Lighting :				
Aquarium Walls				
Other Component				

NOTES : ....

....

....

....

Tank : .... Date : ....

Fish Count : .... Feeding : ....

FRESHWATER PARAMETERS

Water Temperature :	Nitrate Level :
pH Level :	Magnesium :
Ammonia :	Alkalinity : (Carbonate Hardness)
Nitrite Level :	Phosphates :
Calcium Level :	Water Change — 10 - 15 % of water / 20 - 25 % of water
Salinity Level :	Other Condition :

TANK EQUIPMENT CHECK

COMPONENT	STATUS	CLEANING DATE	REPLACEMENT DATE	OBSERVATIONS
Filters :				
Pumps :				
Heaters :				
Lighting :				
Aquarium Walls				
Other Component				

NOTES : ....

....

....

....

Tank : .... Date : ....

Fish Count : .... Feeding : ....

FRESHWATER PARAMETERS

Water Temperature :	Nitrate Level :
pH Level :	Magnesium :
Ammonia :	Alkalinity : (Carbonate Hardness)
Nitrite Level :	Phosphates :
Calcium Level :	Water Change — 10 - 15 % of water / 20 - 25 % of water
Salinity Level :	Other Condition :

TANK EQUIPMENT CHECK

COMPONENT	STATUS	CLEANING DATE	REPLACEMENT DATE	OBSERVATIONS
Filters :				
Pumps :				
Heaters :				
Lighting :				
Aquarium Walls				
Other Component				

NOTES : ....

....

....

....

Tank : .... Date : ....

Fish Count : .... Feeding : ....

FRESHWATER PARAMETERS

Water Temperature :	Nitrate Level :
pH Level :	Magnesium :
Ammonia :	Alkalinity : (Carbonate Hardness)
Nitrite Level :	Phosphates :
Calcium Level :	Water Change — 10 - 15 % of water / 20 - 25 % of water
Salinity Level :	Other Condition :

TANK EQUIPMENT CHECK

COMPONENT	STATUS	CLEANING DATE	REPLACEMENT DATE	OBSERVATIONS
Filters :				
Pumps :				
Heaters :				
Lighting :				
Aquarium Walls				
Other Component				

NOTES : ....

....

....

....

Tank : .... Date : ....

Fish Count : .... Feeding : ....

FRESHWATER PARAMETERS

Water Temperature :	Nitrate Level :
pH Level :	Magnesium :
Ammonia :	Alkalinity : (Carbonate Hardness)
Nitrite Level :	Phosphates :
Calcium Level :	Water Change — 10 - 15 % of water / 20 - 25 % of water
Salinity Level :	Other Condition :

TANK EQUIPMENT CHECK

COMPONENT	STATUS	CLEANING DATE	REPLACEMENT DATE	OBSERVATIONS
Filters :				
Pumps :				
Heaters :				
Lighting :				
Aquarium Walls				
Other Component				

NOTES : ....

....

....

....

Tank : .... Date : ....

Fish Count : .... Feeding : ....

FRESHWATER PARAMETERS

Water Temperature :	Nitrate Level :
pH Level :	Magnesium :
Ammonia :	Alkalinity : (Carbonate Hardness)
Nitrite Level :	Phosphates :
Calcium Level :	Water Change / 10 - 15 % of water / 20 - 25 % of water
Salinity Level :	Other Condition :

TANK EQUIPMENT CHECK

COMPONENT	STATUS	CLEANING DATE	REPLACEMENT DATE	OBSERVATIONS
Filters :				
Pumps :				
Heaters :				
Lighting :				
Aquarium Walls				
Other Component				

NOTES : ....

....

....

....

Tank : .... Date : ....

Fish Count : .... Feeding : ....

FRESHWATER PARAMETERS

Water Temperature :	Nitrate Level :
pH Level :	Magnesium :
Ammonia :	Alkalinity : (Carbonate Hardness)
Nitrite Level :	Phosphates :
Calcium Level :	Water Change — 10 - 15 % of water / 20 - 25 % of water
Salinity Level :	Other Condition :

TANK EQUIPMENT CHECK

COMPONENT	STATUS	CLEANING DATE	REPLACEMENT DATE	OBSERVATIONS
Filters :				
Pumps :				
Heaters :				
Lighting :				
Aquarium Walls				
Other Component				

NOTES : ....

....

....

....

Tank : .... Date : ....

Fish Count : .... Feeding : ....

FRESHWATER PARAMETERS

Water Temperature :	Nitrate Level :
pH Level :	Magnesium :
Ammonia :	Alkalinity : (Carbonate Hardness)
Nitrite Level :	Phosphates :
Calcium Level :	Water Change 10 - 15 % of water 20 - 25 % of water
Salinity Level :	Other Condition :

TANK EQUIPMENT CHECK

COMPONENT	STATUS	CLEANING DATE	REPLACEMENT DATE	OBSERVATIONS
Filters :				
Pumps :				
Heaters :				
Lighting :				
Aquarium Walls				
Other Component				

NOTES : ....

....

....

....

Tank : .... Date : ....

Fish Count : .... Feeding : ....

FRESHWATER PARAMETERS

Water Temperature :	Nitrate Level :
pH Level :	Magnesium :
Ammonia :	Alkalinity : (Carbonate Hardness)
Nitrite Level :	Phosphates :
Calcium Level :	Water Change — 10 - 15 % of water / 20 - 25 % of water
Salinity Level :	Other Condition :

TANK EQUIPMENT CHECK

COMPONENT	STATUS	CLEANING DATE	REPLACEMENT DATE	OBSERVATIONS
Filters :				
Pumps :				
Heaters :				
Lighting :				
Aquarium Walls				
Other Component				

NOTES : ....

....

....

....

Tank : .... Date : ....

Fish Count : .... Feeding : ....

FRESHWATER PARAMETERS

Water Temperature :	Nitrate Level :
pH Level :	Magnesium :
Ammonia :	Alkalinity : (Carbonate Hardness)
Nitrite Level :	Phosphates :
Calcium Level :	Water Change — 10 - 15 % of water / 20 - 25 % of water
Salinity Level :	Other Condition :

TANK EQUIPMENT CHECK

COMPONENT	STATUS	CLEANING DATE	REPLACEMENT DATE	OBSERVATIONS
Filters :				
Pumps :				
Heaters :				
Lighting :				
Aquarium Walls				
Other Component				

NOTES : ....

....

....

....

Tank : .... Date : ....

Fish Count : .... Feeding : ....

FRESHWATER PARAMETERS

Water Temperature :	Nitrate Level :
pH Level :	Magnesium :
Ammonia :	Alkalinity : (Carbonate Hardness)
Nitrite Level :	Phosphates :
Calcium Level :	Water Change — 10 - 15 % of water / 20 - 25 % of water
Salinity Level :	Other Condition :

TANK EQUIPMENT CHECK

COMPONENT	STATUS	CLEANING DATE	REPLACEMENT DATE	OBSERVATIONS
Filters :				
Pumps :				
Heaters :				
Lighting :				
Aquarium Walls				
Other Component				

NOTES : ....

....

....

....

Tank : .... Date : ....

Fish Count : .... Feeding : ....

FRESHWATER PARAMETERS

Water Temperature :	Nitrate Level :
pH Level :	Magnesium :
Ammonia :	Alkalinity : (Carbonate Hardness)
Nitrite Level :	Phosphates :
Calcium Level :	Water Change — 10 - 15 % of water 20 - 25 % of water
Salinity Level :	Other Condition :

TANK EQUIPMENT CHECK

COMPONENT	STATUS	CLEANING DATE	REPLACEMENT DATE	OBSERVATIONS
Filters :				
Pumps :				
Heaters :				
Lighting :				
Aquarium Walls				
Other Component				

NOTES : ....

....

....

....

Tank : .... Date : ....

Fish Count : .... Feeding : ....

FRESHWATER PARAMETERS

Water Temperature :	Nitrate Level :
pH Level :	Magnesium :
Ammonia :	Alkalinity : (Carbonate Hardness)
Nitrite Level :	Phosphates :
Calcium Level :	Water Change — 10 - 15 % of water / 20 - 25 % of water
Salinity Level :	Other Condition :

TANK EQUIPMENT CHECK

COMPONENT	STATUS	CLEANING DATE	REPLACEMENT DATE	OBSERVATIONS
Filters :				
Pumps :				
Heaters :				
Lighting :				
Aquarium Walls				
Other Component				

NOTES : ....

....

....

....

Tank : .... Date : ....

Fish Count : .... Feeding : ....

FRESHWATER PARAMETERS

Water Temperature :	Nitrate Level :
pH Level :	Magnesium :
Ammonia :	Alkalinity : (Carbonate Hardness)
Nitrite Level :	Phosphates :
Calcium Level :	Water Change — 10 - 15 % of water / 20 - 25 % of water
Salinity Level :	Other Condition :

TANK EQUIPMENT CHECK

COMPONENT	STATUS	CLEANING DATE	REPLACEMENT DATE	OBSERVATIONS
Filters :				
Pumps :				
Heaters :				
Lighting :				
Aquarium Walls				
Other Component				

NOTES : ....

....

....

....

Tank : ....   Date : ....

Fish Count : ....   Feeding : ....

FRESHWATER PARAMETERS

Water Temperature :	Nitrate Level :
pH Level :	Magnesium :
Ammonia :	Alkalinity : (Carbonate Hardness)
Nitrite Level :	Phosphates :
Calcium Level :	Water Change — 10 - 15 % of water / 20 - 25 % of water
Salinity Level :	Other Condition :

TANK EQUIPMENT CHECK

COMPONENT	STATUS	CLEANING DATE	REPLACEMENT DATE	OBSERVATIONS
Filters :				
Pumps :				
Heaters :				
Lighting :				
Aquarium Walls				
Other Component				

NOTES : ....

....

....

....

Tank : .... Date : ....

Fish Count : .... Feeding : ....

FRESHWATER PARAMETERS

Water Temperature :	Nitrate Level :
pH Level :	Magnesium :
Ammonia :	Alkalinity : (Carbonate Hardness)
Nitrite Level :	Phosphates :
Calcium Level :	Water Change — 10 - 15 % of water / 20 - 25 % of water
Salinity Level :	Other Condition :

TANK EQUIPMENT CHECK

COMPONENT	STATUS	CLEANING DATE	REPLACEMENT DATE	OBSERVATIONS
Filters :				
Pumps :				
Heaters :				
Lighting :				
Aquarium Walls				
Other Component				

NOTES : ....

....

....

....

Tank : .... Date : ....

Fish Count : .... Feeding : ....

FRESHWATER PARAMETERS

Water Temperature :	Nitrate Level :
pH Level :	Magnesium :
Ammonia :	Alkalinity : (Carbonate Hardness)
Nitrite Level :	Phosphates :
Calcium Level :	Water Change — 10 - 15 % of water / 20 - 25 % of water
Salinity Level :	Other Condition :

TANK EQUIPMENT CHECK

COMPONENT	STATUS	CLEANING DATE	REPLACEMENT DATE	OBSERVATIONS
Filters :				
Pumps :				
Heaters :				
Lighting :				
Aquarium Walls				
Other Component				

NOTES : ....

....

....

....

Tank : .... Date : ....

Fish Count : .... Feeding : ....

FRESHWATER PARAMETERS	
Water Temperature :	Nitrate Level :
pH Level :	Magnesium :
Ammonia :	Alkalinity : (Carbonate Hardness)
Nitrite Level :	Phosphates :
Calcium Level :	Water Change / 10 - 15 % of water / 20 - 25 % of water
Salinity Level :	Other Condition :

TANK EQUIPMENT CHECK

COMPONENT	STATUS	CLEANING DATE	REPLACEMENT DATE	OBSERVATIONS
Filters :				
Pumps :				
Heaters :				
Lighting :				
Aquarium Walls				
Other Component				

NOTES : ....

....

....

....

Tank : ....   Date : ....

Fish Count : ....   Feeding : ....

FRESHWATER PARAMETERS

Water Temperature :	Nitrate Level :
pH Level :	Magnesium :
Ammonia :	Alkalinity : (Carbonate Hardness)
Nitrite Level :	Phosphates :
Calcium Level :	Water Change / 10 - 15 % of water / 20 - 25 % of water
Salinity Level :	Other Condition :

TANK EQUIPMENT CHECK

COMPONENT	STATUS	CLEANING DATE	REPLACEMENT DATE	OBSERVATIONS
Filters :				
Pumps :				
Heaters :				
Lighting :				
Aquarium Walls				
Other Component				

NOTES : ....

....

....

....

Tank : .... Date : ....

Fish Count : .... Feeding : ....

FRESHWATER PARAMETERS

Water Temperature :	Nitrate Level :
pH Level :	Magnesium :
Ammonia :	Alkalinity : (Carbonate Hardness)
Nitrite Level :	Phosphates :
Calcium Level :	Water Change — 10 - 15 % of water / 20 - 25 % of water
Salinity Level :	Other Condition :

TANK EQUIPMENT CHECK

COMPONENT	STATUS	CLEANING DATE	REPLACEMENT DATE	OBSERVATIONS
Filters :				
Pumps :				
Heaters :				
Lighting :				
Aquarium Walls				
Other Component				

NOTES : ....

....

....

....

Tank : .... Date : ....

Fish Count : .... Feeding : ....

FRESHWATER PARAMETERS

Water Temperature :	Nitrate Level :
pH Level :	Magnesium :
Ammonia :	Alkalinity : (Carbonate Hardness)
Nitrite Level :	Phosphates :
Calcium Level :	Water Change — 10 - 15 % of water 20 - 25 % of water
Salinity Level :	Other Condition :

TANK EQUIPMENT CHECK

COMPONENT	STATUS	CLEANING DATE	REPLACEMENT DATE	OBSERVATIONS
Filters :				
Pumps :				
Heaters :				
Lighting :				
Aquarium Walls				
Other Component				

NOTES : ....

....

....

....

Tank : ....   Date : ....

Fish Count : ....   Feeding : ....

FRESHWATER PARAMETERS

Water Temperature :	Nitrate Level :
pH Level :	Magnesium :
Ammonia :	Alkalinity : (Carbonate Hardness)
Nitrite Level :	Phosphates :
Calcium Level :	Water Change — 10 - 15 % of water / 20 - 25 % of water
Salinity Level :	Other Condition :

TANK EQUIPMENT CHECK

COMPONENT	STATUS	CLEANING DATE	REPLACEMENT DATE	OBSERVATIONS
Filters :				
Pumps :				
Heaters :				
Lighting :				
Aquarium Walls				
Other Component				

NOTES : ....

....

....

....

Made in the USA
Monee, IL
10 December 2021

84558377R00072